TAYLOR SWIFT

First published in the UK in 2019 by Studio Press Books,
an imprint of Bonnier Books UK
The Plaza, 535 King's Road, London, SW10 0SZ
www.studiopressbooks.co.uk
www.bonnierbooks.co.uk

© 2019 Studio Press

Written by Melanie Hamm

Cover illustration by Keith Robinson

A CIP catalogue record for this book is available from
the British Library.

Paperback: 978-1-78741-520-1

Printed and bound by Clays Ltd, Elcograf S.p.A

3 5 7 9 10 8 6 4 2

ULTIMATE SUPERSTARS

TAYLOR SWIFT

For Victoria

CONTENTS

CHAPTER 1 - THE SQUAD 9

CHAPTER 2 - A CHRISTMAS BABY 14

CHAPTER 3 - THE CURTAIN GOES UP 21

CHAPTER 4 - THE STAR-SPANGLED BANNER 27

CHAPTER 5 - STONE HARBOR 36

CHAPTER 6 - KARAOKE DREAMS 43

CHAPTER 7 - NASHVILLE 50

CHAPTER 8 - A GUITAR LESSON 57

CHAPTER 9 - NEVER CHANGE WHO YOU ARE 63

CHAPTER 10 - TIM MCGRAW 69

CHAPTER 11 - BIG MACHINE RECORDS 74

CHAPTER 12 - THE WAIT IS OVER 80

CHAPTER 13 – COOKIE POWER 86

CHAPTER 14 – FEARLESS 92

CHAPTER 15 – T-PARTY 98

CHAPTER 16 – GRAMMYS. 105

CHAPTER 17 – THE IMAGINARIUM 114

CHAPTER 18 – SPEAK NOW. 119

CHAPTER 19 – PAYING IT BACK 123

CHAPTER 20 – RED. 129

CHAPTER 21 – FOURTH OF JULY. 138

CHAPTER 22 – BITING BACK 143

CHAPTER 23 – REPUTATION 149

CHAPTER 24 – JINGLE BALL. 156

CHAPTER 1

THE SQUAD

In the middle of Hyde Park, London, a sea of fans stood in the golden summer sunshine watching a huge stage between the trees. Hundreds of colourful homemade signs swayed gently in the breeze. Each one was lovingly decorated with a slogan:

T Swift

Swifty

I Heart Taylor Swift!

Swifties 4Ever.

Some fans had even dressed up as Taylor Swift's famous cats, Olivia and Meredith, the stars of her social media feeds. "We love you, Taylor Swift!" they screamed. "Taylor! Taylor!"

There wasn't long to wait now. The noise of the crowd got steadily louder, excited whoops and cheers filling the air.

Suddenly – dressed in a blue metallic skater skirt, green sequinned jacket and white-rimmed shades – Taylor appeared onstage. Screams rippled through the audience like a Mexican wave. Hyde Park was ready!

As the first notes of 'Welcome to New York' floated across the park, the singer's image appeared on three vast screens. The crowd was on its feet now, holding their signs high, hugging their friends, dancing, and singing along with the familiar lyrics.

Onstage, Taylor smiled at her huge Hyde Park audience. She had travelled the world many times over, but London would always have a special place in her heart. Above her was a perfect summer sky, bright blue and dotted with fluffy clouds. Ancient, green trees towered on either side of her. Just out of sight was historical Kensington Palace. Yes, London was magical.

And today, 28 June, 2015, 65,000 people had turned up to share it with her. This crowd was bigger than it would be in most of the stadiums she had played in. The audience stretched further than Taylor could see.

As she sang – hit after hit from her new album, *1989* – the bright afternoon sunshine faded into twilight. The beautiful park was silhouetted against a dusty golden sunset. Floodlights fired into life, beaming down onto the stage, lighting the trees on either side with an ethereal glow and making the sequins of Taylor's silver dress shimmer. She had already changed costume three times!

Taylor had just sung 'Love Story', supported by her amazing troupe of twelve dancers and four backing singers. Her audience waved their phones, the lights glimmering in the darkness. How romantic it was, thought Taylor. The perfect setting for her most romantic song.

But it was time to switch things up.

"London, England, Hyde Park," announced Taylor, "please welcome to the stage one of your own, Miss Cara Delevingne..."

Onto the stage walked the model Cara Delevingne. She was waving a huge Union Jack.

The crowd went wild. And that wasn't all... Behind Cara came the models Kendall Jenner, Karlie Kloss, Gigi Hadid and Martha Hunt, and the tennis player Serena Williams.

"These are my friends!" said Taylor, grinning.

Together they strode along the catwalk stage, then stood arm in arm to sing 'Style'. Taylor's fans knew how important friendship was to her. These women were more than A-list party pals – they were her Squad. Her mates. Her BFFs. Her besties. They were the people she turned to when she needed advice and support, and to share her joys and sadnesses.

Who else but Taylor Swift would fill a stage with friends?

Taylor's final song was 'Shake It Off', a fan favourite. The video for the song featured some of her own fans dancing alongside professionals. Here, in the middle of the park, the crowd was part of the action too. Taylor danced at the end of a mechanical bridge that stretched into the audience like a crane, hovering just above their heads. The star was almost close enough to touch!

And the Swifties joined in, belting the anthem into the night – 65,000 people singing as one. The stage in front of them was lit like a kaleidoscope of magical, changing colours, while above them the London sky was a clear, deep indigo. It was an evening they knew they would never forget.

And Taylor wouldn't either.

CHAPTER 2

A CHRISTMAS BABY

Andrea and Scott Swift had been married for just over a year when Andrea discovered she was pregnant with their first child. Like her husband, thirty-year-old Andrea worked in finance. With a great career and a wonderful new husband, life was good. And now a baby was on the way! It felt like the perfect next step in the couple's life together.

The Swifts lived in West Reading, Pennsylvania, near where Scott had grown up. Their home was big and comfortable, and Andrea and Scott had fun preparing it for the new arrival. There was a nursery to decorate. A crib to build. Baby clothes to buy.

And to add to the excitement, Christmas was

coming. The Swifts were well prepared, of course. From the first week of December, a huge tree sparkled in the living room. Fairy lights hung from the windows, and on every surface stood cards from friends and family. Would the baby come before the big day? Andrea hoped so. How magical it would be to celebrate Christmas as a family this year!

On 13 December, 1989, less than two weeks before Christmas, Taylor Alison Swift was born.

"Oh," breathed Andrea, as the nurses gently placed the tiny infant into her arms. The baby had her mother's big, blue eyes, fringed with sandy lashes. Her cheeks were rosy red and her head was dusted with fine blonde hair. "She's gorgeous!"

"Like a little princess," added Scott proudly.

All around them, the Brampton Civic Hospital bustled with activity. But as Andrea and Scott huddled over their newborn daughter, nothing else in the world mattered. Finally they were parents – to the tiniest, most perfect little person on earth.

It hardly seemed real.

Back home, though, caring for a baby was very

real indeed – and their newborn daughter knew just how to get what she wanted! Under the glow of the Christmas lights, Scott and Andrea fed her, changed her, rocked her till she slept... then started all over again as soon as she woke. Which was often!

Friends and family arrived, bringing Christmas greetings, gifts and cuddles, helping with the nappy changes, and fetching fresh clothing. And, of course, everyone wanted to know what Scott and Andrea had decided to call their baby.

"Taylor," announced Andrea, grinning. "She'll thank us when she's older!"

Scott explained. "When she applies for jobs, no one will be able to tell whether she's male or female. If she becomes a stockbroker, it'll help her, believe me!"

It seemed so early to be considering Taylor's career, but Andrea and Scott had been thinking about this important decision for months. Scott was a stockbroker. He and Andrea knew how hard it was for women to succeed in some careers – including finance. It they could help their daughter over that first hurdle, they were determined to do so.

"Plus 'Taylor Swift' has a ring to it," added Andrea, stroking little Taylor on the cheek. "Don't you think so, baby Tay?"

Christmas came and went, in a whirl of presents, feasting, cuddles and sleepless nights. The months of January and February followed, dark and cold. Then, eventually, signs of spring began to appear outside.

Andrea and Scott's new home in Pennsylvania was on a Christmas-tree farm. Behind the house were eleven acres of beautiful countryside, including a fruit orchard, a hayloft and of course a large forest of fir trees, ready to be cut down and sold when Christmas came round. Andrea and Scott had lived in the city for most of their lives, and they wanted to raise their family surrounded by nature. How wonderful the countryside around them looked as spring began to flourish!

As she grew, little Taylor loved to toddle around the farm, jumping in the hay, splashing in puddles and chasing the barn cats, who were always too fast for her. Andrea also kept horses, including a friendly Shetland pony called Ginger, and Taylor had her first pony ride at just nine months, sitting securely on her mother's lap.

"Would you like to stroke his mane?" Andrea asked. She could see Taylor was fascinated by the placid pony.

Taylor reached forwards and clutched a tiny fistful of Ginger's tan-coloured mane. She gurgled with delight.

"Taylor, can you say 'Ginger'?" asked Andrea. "Ginger. Ginger."

"Gi-gi!"

"Well done!" Andrea grinned. It was so exciting watching her little daughter grow and learn. Taylor was so smart. Every day she was picking up new words.

"You'll be talking in no time, won't you, baby Tay?" laughed Andrea.

Three years later, Taylor's brother, Austin, was born. As soon as he was old enough to totter around the farm, Tay introduced him to all her favourite places. Playing on the farm was even more fun, now that Tay had someone else to do it with. Together, the two children rode on the tractor, picked fruit in the orchard and made forts in the hayloft. To Taylor and Austin, it was paradise.

Taylor used her imagination to tell stories about the creatures that lived on the farm and in the wood – particularly the barn cats, and the mice and birds they preyed on. Every time she found a dead creature, killed by the cats, it gave her an idea for a tale. The more gruesome, the better!

"Please don't scare Austin," warned Andrea. "He's only little!"

Alongside their daughter's passion for storytelling, Taylor's parents had also noticed her love of singing. She had an astonishing ability to remember words and tunes.

"It's extraordinary," Andrea told Scott one day. "We went to the cinema this afternoon, and when we came out, Taylor had memorised every single song. Every word. Every note."

Scott frowned.

"She must have heard them before, surely?" he asked.

"She hadn't," said Andrea. "We saw a Disney movie. It has only just been released. I'd never heard them before either."

"I guess singing is in her blood," said Scott.

"True!" Andrea laughed.

Andrea's mother, Marjorie, had been an opera singer. Taylor's grandmother had performed all over the world, from East Asia to South America. Now in her sixties, Marjorie still had a beautiful voice, and Taylor loved to hear her sing when they went to church together every Sunday. Perhaps Taylor had inherited some of her grandmother's talent?

Her parents knew it was still too early to tell. Taylor was good at so many things, after all: telling stories, writing poems, drawing. And whenever grown-ups asked her what she wanted to be when she was older, young Taylor always gave the same answer: "A stockbroker! Like Dad!"

CHAPTER 3

THE CURTAIN GOES UP

There was an excited hush in the audience. Nine-year-old Taylor sat between her mum and brother Austin, her eyes fixed on the stage. The overture had finished, and the lights had gone down. Taylor squeezed her mum's hand tightly. In just a few seconds, the curtain would rise. She could hardly contain her excitement!

Slowly, the heavy velvet curtains parted, and the stage lights began to glow with magical blues and purples. The Berks Youth Theater Academy's production of *Charlie and the Chocolate Factory* was beginning. In the middle of the stage was a large, iron bed. Charlie's four grandparents were packed into it. The bed was the only place to keep warm –

Taylor knew that from the book. The grandparents were played by children – all the characters were – but it didn't matter. This was theatre, and Taylor was gripped.

As the show went on, the rest of the characters took to the stage: Augustus Gloop, Violet Beauregarde, Veruca Salt, Mike TeaVee, the Oompa Loompas and Willy Wonka himself. Some of the children performing were older than Taylor, some were younger. How good they were – not just at acting, but at singing too. And it looked like they were having so much fun!

As the first half ended, applause rang around the theatre. Taylor blinked with surprise as the house lights came up.

"Taylor! Earth to Taylor!" laughed Andrea. "Are you enjoying the show?"

Enjoying it? Taylor had been transported. She could hardly wait for the second half to begin. She could feel a tug in her chest – she wished more than anything that she could be up onstage with them.

"Momma, I want to be in a show!" she cried. "Can I audition for something? Please!"

Andrea smiled. She was happy that Taylor was interested. It had been a difficult few months for her daughter. The Swifts had recently moved from their idyllic farm in the countryside to the nearby town of Wyomissing. Taylor was struggling to settle in. She missed her friends, and the kids in her new school weren't exactly welcoming. Taylor had returned home in tears several times that week.

Tay's classmates made fun of her good grades, her clothes and, most of all, her love of country music; LeAnn Rimes, Shania Twain, the Dixie Chicks... Taylor listened to nothing else. But country wasn't cool – and the other kids let Taylor know it, loud and clear. Andrea thought that youth theatre would appeal to Taylor's creative side, and she hoped her daughter would make some new friends. Friends who understood her. She was delighted Taylor wanted to get involved.

"There are auditions for *Annie* next week," she said, giving her daughter a hug. "I saw a notice. Do you remember *Annie*? We saw the film."

"Next week? That's so soon!" squeaked Taylor nervously. "I need more time to practise!"

"You have plenty of time, honey," said Andrea. "You're singing constantly!"

It was true. At home, at school, on holiday – Taylor was always singing, always performing.

But when the evening of the audition came round, Taylor felt sick with nerves. She knew she could sing, and she was pretty sure she could act too. No, there was another reason for her anxiety. At nine, Taylor was tall for her age. She towered over most of her classmates – and she was dismayed to find that she was the tallest at the audition. Looking around the room, all Taylor could see was other kids staring at her.

Andrea squeezed her hand. "You think they're staring at you," she whispered. "But they're not. They probably think you're staring at *them*!"

Taylor looked up gratefully at her mum. Andrea always noticed what was troubling her. She always made things better.

By the time it was her turn to perform, Taylor's smile, and her confidence, had returned. Everyone clapped once she'd finished singing. Would she be good enough though? There were some very polished performances!

"We'll ring you," said the director.

Taylor spent an anxious week waiting for Andrea to receive a call from the director. Finally, it came. Taylor had been offered a part! Not a main role, but a part nonetheless. It was a first step. She was going to be onstage!

Rehearsals for Annie started almost immediately. Just as Andrea had hoped, Tay found it easier to make friends here than at school. She loved being around kids who shared her passion for performing.

Most of the other children had been in a show before. They knew exactly what to do when the director called "Stage right!" or "Upstage!". Taylor had a lot to learn, but she threw herself into it with her usual enthusiasm.

And when the week of the show finally came round? It just as thrilling as Tay had imagined. Her part in Annie might be small, but for a few minutes, she felt like a star. It was magical to be standing on a proper stage, in front of hundreds of people, with the applause ringing in her ears.

The next show was *The Sound of Music*. Taylor loved the film, starring Julie Andrews as the young nun, Maria. How amazing it would be to get the lead role!

When the auditions came round, Taylor shone. Now that she had made friends, she no longer worried about being too tall. She didn't feel gawky or awkward. The director was impressed by her clear, sweet singing voice and by the way she looked after the younger children who were auditioning to play the Von Trapp children.

"I got the part!" shrieked Taylor, when she returned home from the audition. "The director told me straight away! I'm going to play Maria!"

"Maria? That's incredible, honey!" Andrea and Scott were almost as excited as Taylor – their daughter's first starring role! They were so proud... and they were also relieved. Taylor had been so unhappy. Seeing her find something she loved to do – and a group of friends she felt comfortable with – was the best feeling in the world.

CHAPTER 4

THE STAR-SPANGLED BANNER

Rehearsals began at once.

Maria was a huge role. Taylor highlighted all her lines in her script – she was in almost every scene and had several solos to sing! Every evening after school, she read and reread her words. In just a few weeks, they were stuck firmly in her head.

Her fellow cast members were amazed.

"You know your lines already?" they asked.

The other kids were still learning their parts. Taylor knew her schoolmates would have made fun of her for studying so hard. But her theatre friends were different.

"I've practised a lot – that's all!" Taylor smiled. "I'll help you with your parts, if you like."

As the show got nearer and nearer, two weekly rehearsals became three. By now, the whole cast had memorised every word and every note. They knew exactly where to stand, and even the dance routines were choreographed to perfection. It was a lot of fun too!

The director was delighted.

"It's sounding really great, kids. All you need now is an audience!"

First though, there was the costume fitting. Taylor needed several outfits to play Maria – and suddenly, she found that being tall was a good thing...

"Everything fits you like a dream!" said the wardrobe mistress. "It's harder with the smaller kids – I have a lot of sewing to do." She handed Taylor a long black robe. "This is your nun's habit. Try it on."

As Taylor stood in front of the mirror, the wardrobe mistress placed a black veil over her head – her nun's headdress. She giggled. She really did look like Maria!

Finally the opening night came around.

Backstage, the cast waited for the lights to go down. Some of the performers were excited. Some were anxious. Most were both!

Dressed in her nun's habit, Taylor couldn't wait to be out onstage. The theatre was packed. All her friends' families were in the audience – and so were Andrea, Scott and Austin. As the house lights went down and the auditorium was plunged into darkness, Taylor felt a flutter of nerves in her stomach.

Then the curtain rose – the show had begun!

The Sound of Music was a triumph. Every performer shone in their role – and Taylor most of all. She wowed the audience with her dazzling singing and the quality of her acting. When the actors took their bows at the end of the show, Taylor got a standing ovation.

"You deserved it!" said the director afterwards. "You've worked so hard, Tay."

Taylor grinned. It hadn't felt like hard work. She had loved every second of it. And she longed to take part in another show.

"Did you see that we're putting on *Grease* next?" asked the director. "Are you going to audition?"

"Yes!" Taylor knew most of the songs from the film already: 'Summer Nights', 'You're the One That I Want', 'Hopelessly Devoted to You'... She couldn't wait.

Grease was full of great roles, and with her brilliant singing voice, ten-year-old Taylor was a natural choice for the lead character, Sandy. The role had several solos and a couple of duets too. Once again, Taylor learned her parts almost straight away.

This time, the director had noticed something about Taylor's performance.

"You're singing Sandy's songs with a country twang, Taylor. You like country music, don't you?"

Tay nodded. LeAnn Rimes, Shania Twain and Faith Hill were her heroes. Happily, the kids here didn't make fun of her musical tastes, like her classmates did. Everyone in the group liked something different.

"Well, don't change a thing. It's sounding fantastic." The director smiled. "In fact, I've got a surprise for you. See how you like the idea of this..."

The Berks Youth Theater group had been asked to sing a *Grease* medley as part of a pre-match warm-up show for the Reading Phillies, the local baseball team. The performance would feature the whole cast, with Taylor in her starring role as Sandy.

"We'll be singing to a whole stadium?" Taylor gasped. "Including solos?"

In the theatre, they performed for hundreds of people, at most – but this performance would be in front of thousands!

"Exactly." The director smiled. "The stadium seats nine thousand. It'll be quite an audience!"

It was 8 August, 2000, the evening of the stadium performance. The sun was setting and the floodlights had just come on. The air smelled of hot dogs and fried onions. Taylor and her friends were gathered on the touchline. Many of them came to baseball games with their parents. They were used to sitting up in the stands – not to standing down here by the pitch. What would it feel like to be out there in the middle of the arena?

Suddenly the director hushed them.

"Girls! Boys! It's time!"

Just as they had practised, Taylor led the group to the centre of the field, where they took their opening positions. Each of the singers had a mic, to help their voices carry in the huge space. Over the loudspeaker, the intro music filled the stadium, and Taylor began to sing. She looked over at the touchline where Andrea, Scott and Austin were watching. If only they knew how amazing this felt!

The group was note-perfect as they performed the *Grease* medley. Phew!

Applause rippled through the stadium as they ran off the pitch. The next act was already running on, to continue the 50s-themed show.

"Good job, everyone!" called the director as they tumbled back onto the touchline. "Taylor, come over here, please." She gestured to where the Swifts were standing, with a man Taylor didn't recognise.

Tay gulped. Had she made a mistake? She thought she had sung well – but perhaps she hadn't. The director was smiling, though, and so too were her parents. What was going on?

It was Andrea who explained. "Taylor, this is Mr Hunsicker, the stadium manager. He would like your help."

Taylor looked puzzled. Help? How could she possibly help at a baseball match? She was the least sporty person she knew!

The man in the suit smiled at her. "My anthem singer hasn't turned up. I need a replacement – and quickly. I'm hoping you could sing in her place, Miss Swift."

Sing the national anthem, by herself? Wow!

"I've just heard your *Grease* medley. You've got a terrific voice. Do you think you can help me out?"

Taylor's heart was pounding. The national anthem, 'The Star-Spangled Banner', was sung before every American sports match. All the players would be on the pitch. The Phillies' mascot too. It would be a huge moment.

She looked at Andrea, who nodded. "You can do it, honey!"

"Yes! Yes, I'll do it," said Taylor.

"You've got fifteen minutes to prepare," said Mr Hunsicker.

So, with Andrea at her side, Taylor rehearsed the words of the national anthem. She mustn't make a mistake, out there in front of this massive crowd! But Taylor's memory for words had always been good.

"You've got this," whispered Andrea, giving her one last hug.

Back on the touchline, Taylor gazed up at the stands. They were full now. Thousands of people were staring down at her. Taylor felt as tiny as an ant. Her heart was trembling in her chest. Her fingers were trembling too! Was this really happening?

Suddenly the teams – the Reading Phillies and their opponents – came striding onto the field. They were led by the Phillies' mascot, Screwball, a giant baseball wearing a red cap. Mr Hunsicker put a hand on Taylor's shoulder, and together they followed the teams out onto the pitch.

"Please rise, and remove your hats..." came the announcement over the loudspeaker.

Out there in the darkness beyond the floodlights, the whole stadium rose as one.

"Here, to honour America with the singing of our national anthem..."

Taylor's mouth felt dry. She tried to swallow, but there was no moisture. She blinked. A bead of nervous sweat trickled down her forehead.

"... is ten-year-old Taylor Swift."

For an instant there was utter and complete silence. The only thing Taylor could hear was her own breath.

Then, without thinking, she opened her mouth and the familiar notes came flying out. She had no idea if they were in the right order or not!

On the touchline, Andrea and Scott's hearts swelled with pride, as their daughter's crystal-clear voice rang through the arena.

A minute disappeared in a flash – and suddenly the stadium erupted in applause.

Taylor's unexpected solo was over.

CHAPTER 5

STONE HARBOR

"I can see it!" shouted Taylor. "I can see it!"

Every summer since Taylor was two years old, the Swift family had been making the same drive from their home in Pennsylvania to the beach town of Stone Harbor, New Jersey.

And every year Taylor and Austin competed for who would be first to spot their beautiful white holiday house, as it came into view on the coast road.

Taylor's heart always soared as they approached. Stone Harbor was the place she loved most in the world. She loved their comfortable home, with its huge windows overlooking the water. She loved her cosy 'clubroom' above the garage, painted in her favourite colours. She loved the white, sandy beach, the sound of the waves and the smell of the sea, the fiery sunsets and the star-filled night skies.

She loved the wildlife too – the seabirds that swooped over the estuary, the family of otters that had made a home on the wooden dock just behind their house. Sometimes she even saw dolphins swimming in the bay! Most of all, though, she loved the constant stream of friends, old and new, flowing in and out of the Swifts' welcoming seafront house. There was always something fun to do – water sports, sailing, swimming, visiting the ice-cream parlour, or just lazing on the beach – and there was always someone awesome to do it with.

Yes, Stone Harbor was magical.

Ten-year-old Taylor felt at her most creative on her long, sunny summer holidays. She loved to write – it was one of the things that made her happiest – and here in Stone Harbor, her imagination took flight. She filled her notebooks with stories, poems and songs – especially songs! Her subjects? Everything... Her friends. Boys. School. Her dreams. Her worries. There was nothing Taylor didn't write about.

Up till now, the only audience for Tay's songs had been her friends and family. This year, though, Taylor had a mission.

It was mid-morning, and already the summer sun was beating down on Stone Harbor. With a determined look on her face, Taylor headed towards Ocean Drive, the bustling main street. The smell of waffles and fresh coffee hung in the air; the cafes and restaurants were already busy with people drinking coffee and shakes, and eating delicious ice-cream sundaes.

Here goes...

Taylor pushed open the door of the first coffee shop she came to and put on her brightest smile.

"My name's Taylor Swift. Can I sing in your shop today?" she asked the woman behind the counter. "I've got a ton of songs."

The woman frowned.

"I'm sorry," came the answer. "We're just too busy, honey. Why don't you try next door?"

Taylor looked around. The cafe was packed. There was barely room to squeeze between the tables. She thanked the woman and hurried to the next coffee shop.

But the answer there was the same: too busy.

"Look, there's no room for you to sit!" the owner told her. "I can't give you a space that I could give to a customer."

Taylor smiled politely. "Thanks anyway."

"Why don't you try Coffee Talk on 97th Street?" suggested the owner. "They often have live music."

So Taylor headed for Coffee Talk. If she had to, she would ask in every single coffee shop in town!

Coffee Talk was cosy inside. There were long wooden benches scattered with red cushions, comfy armchairs, bookcases heaving under the weight of books, and floor lamps with pretty vintage shades. The walls were papered in yellowing newsprint, and there were more types of coffee chalked on the board than Taylor had ever seen in her life.

Taylor took a deep breath.

"I'm just wondering if I could sing here sometime?" she asked the manager. "My name's Taylor Swift, and I'm pretty good. At least, other people say I am."

The manager smiled.

"Well, let's hear what you've got, Taylor." She settled herself on a stool and gestured for Taylor to take the one next to her.

Taylor knew exactly what to sing – the song closest to her heart, 'Invisible'. She had written it about the boy who lived next door to the Swift's holiday home. Most days, he came round and sat in her clubroom, telling her about the girl that he liked. He never noticed how much Taylor liked him, and she knew he never would. She was completely invisible to him, and it was a horrible feeling.

The coffee-shop manager's eyes widened as Taylor's luminous voice filled the room. She sang a country song, richly melodic. The high notes seemed to float effortlessly into the air, while the low ones lingered, tugging at her heartstrings. The manager hadn't expected to hear a country song from such a young singer. She looked around at her customers. She could see the same question on all their faces: who was this girl?

As Taylor's final notes drifted away, loud applause rang through the room. The manager blinked in disbelief. The girl was extraordinary. She hadn't sung a wrong note. And she knew that the catchy country tune would stick in her mind for hours.

"What did you say your name was, sweetheart?" she asked.

"Taylor Swift."

"And you wrote that song yourself?"

"Yeah," answered Taylor. "I have loads more. That was the best one though!"

The manager looked around the room at the beaming faces of her customers. "Well, Taylor Swift, you can come back and sing whenever you like. We'd love to have you."

Taylor squealed with pleasure. Her first gig! "Thank you!" she said. "Thank you so much." She took a deep breath, drinking in the sweet scent of roasting coffee and muffins. "Can I stay and sing now?"

"Yes! You stay right there and sing for us!" a customer called out.

"Let's have another song!" said another.

"Something upbeat this time!" cried a third.

The manager grinned. "I think you have your answer," she said.

Over that summer, Taylor became a regular at Coffee Talk. She hadn't been exaggerating – she had hundreds of songs, and she was writing new ones all the time. When she ran out of material, she made up lyrics and tunes on the spot, always with a melodic country vibe. There was so much to sing about: spending time with the people she loved, running along the warm, white sands of the bay, the vast ocean that magically changed colour from blue to grey to green to deep, ink-black at night, the seabirds swooping low over the marsh...

Stone Harbor was like a fairy tale, an enchanted place where anything could happen. And performing at Coffee Talk, in front of a clapping, cheering audience? That was the best part of the fairy tale!

CHAPTER 6

KARAOKE DREAMS

By now, Taylor's mind was made up. She didn't want to be a stockbroker – she had never been sure what stockbrokers did anyway. She wanted to be a singer!

Back home in Wyomissing, after the long summer holiday, Taylor made a plan. Her Coffee Talk performances had given her confidence. Now she needed to find bigger audiences. She needed to challenge herself.

It wasn't long before she found the perfect opportunity.

Every week, a big country-music karaoke competition was held at the Pat Garrett Roadhouse in nearby Strausstown. Pat Garrett was a country singer and songwriter who was well known in the area. He had his own band, and his competition attracted country artists from all over Pennsylvania.

Pat was surprised to see such a young singer in the crowd. Did this little blonde girl have what it took to win against the older singers, with all their music experience?

Well, not at first.

Every week, Scott and Andrea drove Taylor to the roadhouse to compete in the karaoke contest. Every week, she was beaten by a more experienced singer. But Taylor was determined. So what, if she didn't win first time? Or second time? Or even fiftieth time?

Pat watched as the young singer returned week after week, month after month, learning from the other singers and improving her performance every time.

That kid has dedication, he thought to himself.

Taylor's passion for country music was clear to see. She hadn't won yet, but there was something about her. A star quality that it was impossible to ignore.

Surely, thought Pat, *it's just a matter of time*.

And it was.

Finally – singing 'Big Deal', by her hero LeAnn Rimes – Taylor won her first competition.

"I've never seen any singer work as hard as this young lady," said Pat, beckoning Taylor to the stage. "Do you want to know your prize, Taylor? You're going to open a gig for Charlie Daniels!"

Charlie Daniels! Taylor could hardly believe her ears. Charlie was one of the biggest names in country music. He had tens of millions of fans, and a star on the Music City Walk of Fame in Nashville. She would be sharing the stage with a legend!

A few weeks later, at the end of September 2001, Taylor Alison Swift walked onstage at the Bloomsburg County Fair for her very first proper gig. Pat Garrett and his band were there, accompanying her on drums and guitars as she sang 'Timber, I'm Falling in Love'. In front of her was an excited crowd of country-music fans. This was the audience she had been dreaming of.

Watching from the crowd, Andrea beamed

with pride. Was this really her little Taylor? Could this be her baby girl, striding across the stage in her cowboy boots, tossing her long, blonde curls and singing with the confidence of an experienced country artist?

Andrea saw the sparkle in her daughter's eyes as she sang, and in that instant she knew Taylor's passion was real and it wasn't going to go away.

Taylor was born to sing.

Together, Andrea and Scott were determined to do everything they could to help Taylor realise her dream. But getting country-music gigs wasn't easy, even for an experienced singer, let alone an eleven-year-old girl. How could they find Taylor the big break that she needed?

Taylor was taking acting and singing lessons from a vocal coach called Kirk Cremer. Kirk ran a sketch comedy group for young people called TheaterKids Live! He was quick to recognise Taylor's talent – especially her flair for comedy – and invited her to join. Tay loved being part of the troupe, improvising comic scenes alongside the other kids. It was so much fun!

And it wasn't long before Kirk had an exciting proposal.

"Would you be interested in going to New York to audition for some Broadway shows?" he asked her. "You've got real talent, Taylor."

Broadway? There was only one possible answer to that question...

"Yes, please!" cried Taylor. "That would be amazing!"

Kirk had selected three other girls to make the trip to New York. He called the group 'Broadway in Training'. He arranged for each of them to have professional photos taken, ready to send to casting directors.

Would this be the opportunity that Taylor had been hoping for?

Soon Taylor and her friends were making regular trips to New York for auditions. Their vocal and acting lessons were giving them new skills and confidence – and eventually it paid off. The girls were offered parts in a film. It would mean time off school, to shoot at a big studio and on location. Tay and her friends were beside themselves with excitement.

But the celebrations were short-lived.

"I'm afraid I have bad news, girls. The film has been cancelled," Kirk told them, just a few weeks later, back in Wyomissing. "It just happens sometimes."

He looked in dismay at the girls' faces. They were crushed. Taylor and her friends had pinned all their hopes on this big break.

"I'm sorry, girls. Really sorry. There will be other opportunities, I promise. We'll keep on going to New York."

By now, Taylor could see how hard getting into show business would be. It didn't matter how hard you worked, you had to have good luck too. And she had discovered something else... It was disappointing not to be in a film, but secretly, she knew it wasn't where her heart lay. Being a country-music singer was still her biggest dream.

Lying on the floor of her attic bedroom, Taylor continued to transform the events of her life – her joys and sorrows – into songs. It was like keeping a diary – one that she sang. And when she wasn't writing music, she was listening to it: Shania Twain, LeAnn Rimes, the Dixie Chicks, Dolly Parton, Tim McGraw, Faith Hill... She loved how country music told stories – like a good book or a brilliant film, it carried away her from reality.

It was a world that she longed to be part of.

CHAPTER 7

NASHVILLE

"Mom, Dad, can we move to Nashville? Please?"

Nashville? Taylor's parents looked at each other. Her question had caught them off guard. Nashville? What could they say?

"Oh, honey," said Scott. "We've just settled here in Wyomissing. Don't you like it here?"

Taylor nodded. She loved their big, elegant house and her amazing attic bedroom. "But Nashville's the home of country music," she pleaded. "It's where all the best singers start out."

Taylor had just watched a documentary about Faith Hill, one of her biggest country-music idols. To make it in country music, you had to live in Nashville, Tennessee. You just had to!

"Darling, it's too far," added Andrea. "And what about the theatre group? You'd miss it."

Taylor frowned. It was true. She'd miss her friends. But the thought of becoming a country singer was constantly in her mind. How could she achieve her dream, here in Pennsylvania?

Andrea looked at Scott. She knew exactly what he was thinking. It was great that Taylor was dreaming big... "Here's an idea, sweetheart," she said. "We'll take a trip there. We'll take your CDs. We'll visit the record companies."

Over the past few months, Taylor had been working with Kirk to make a demo CD. They had recorded it at the studio owned by Kirk's brother, Ronnie. Taylor had sung songs by Dolly Parton, the Dixie Chicks, LeAnn Rimes, Shania Twain – and 'Hopelessly Devoted to You' from *Grease*. She was proud of her first recording.

"That would be cool. Thank you!" Taylor smiled. It wasn't the answer she had hoped for – but a trip to Nashville was the next best thing. Tay knew how lucky she was to have parents who supported her. She wanted to make them proud.

So, together, she and Andrea began to plan the trip to Nashville. They booked a hotel and, with Kirk's help, a large stack of CDs were pressed. They printed sleeves with Taylor's picture on the front and the Swifts' phone number on the back. Then Taylor and Andrea sat up late, stuffing CDs and labels into plastic wallets. Taylor's excitement was at fever pitch.

This trip was going to change everything, she could feel it.

A few weeks later, Taylor was standing in the centre of Music Row, Nashville, staring around her with wide eyes. On either side of the street, music venues, music shops, record companies and restaurants stretched as far as she could see. The venues had huge signs outside, in the shapes of guitars, pianos, violins and cowboy hats. Music posters covered every wall, window and mailbox, and above the rooftops towered giant billboards with the faces of the world's biggest country stars.

Everywhere she looked, Taylor could see music, music, music. She squeezed Andrea's hand.

This place was incredible!

"Shall we hand out some CDs, Momma?" Taylor reached into her bag. "Hey there!" she called to a passer-by. "Would you like my CD?"

"Let's go into the record companies first," said Andrea, smiling. "Do you want me to do the talking?"

Taylor shook her head. She knew exactly what she was going to say. She looked at the list that she'd made of record-label addresses. "Look, we're right by BNA."

Taking a deep breath, she pushed open the door.

"My name's Taylor Swift!" she announced, smiling broadly at the woman behind the reception desk. "I'm eleven. I'd like to give you my CD."

The woman smiled and put out her hand. She gave the CD a quick glance.

"Thanks, honey," she said, and put it down in a pile of CDs beside her computer.

"Please listen to it. It's good. I'm good!" said Taylor brightly. "Call me!"

But the phone rang, and the woman answered it without giving her another glance.

Oh. That hadn't gone so well. But Taylor's

optimism wasn't dented. There were hundreds of record labels here in Nashville. She only needed to find *one* that loved her music!

She reached into her bag and pulled out the next CD.

At the next label, the receptionist smiled and listened kindly. She took Taylor's CD and, once again, put it with a stack of others at the end of her desk.

"Someone will listen to these later," she told Taylor.

Taylor began to have a glimmer of doubt. Everyone was friendly, but would they really listen to all those CDs?

By the end of the day, Taylor's smile was beginning to fade. She tried to hold on to the feeling of excitement that had filled her when she arrived. She was on Music Row. In Nashville! But, but...

Andrea put an arm around her daughter, hugging her tight.

"We've done everything we can. We have to be patient now, honey. There are lots of young singers looking for record deals. It's going to take time."

"I know, Mom. But I want this so badly."

Andrea nodded. "I know you do, sweetheart, and I'm so proud of you. Not just for your talent, but for your determination. Right now, though, I think we need a break, don't you? Shall we get some pizza?"

Music Row was even more thrilling after dark. The huge neon signs glowed red, yellow and blue. Taylor could hear the twang of guitars from every doorway. She felt a tingle of excitement travel all the way down her spine. She was tired, but being here in Nashville felt so right. She had the feeling she belonged here.

It was as if Andrea had read her thoughts. "It's just a short trip, honey. But you'll be back in no time, I'm sure of it."

Taylor flashed her a grin. "I hope so, Momma!"

Back in Wyomissing, Taylor and her family waited and hoped. The weeks went by, but still the life-changing phone call that Tay had been dreaming of didn't come. Maybe the trip wasn't going to change everything, after all.

Perhaps I'm just not good enough, thought Taylor. *Perhaps my voice isn't right? Maybe my songs are too ordinary? Maybe they're bad!*

But what was it her mum had said? *There are lots of young singers looking for record deals...*

Of course! Her songs weren't bad. But Nashville was full of wannabe country singers, hundreds of girls just like her. Why hadn't she realised it before? Having a nice voice and good songs wasn't enough. She had to be different. She had to stand out from the crowd.

And she had an idea of how she could do it.

CHAPTER 8

A GUITAR LESSON

When Taylor had been eight, her parents had given her a guitar. Tay had tried to learn, but it wasn't easy. Her fingers had been too small for even a child-sized instrument, and she had given up in frustration after only a few days.

But her old guitar had been sitting, dusty and unloved, in the corner of her bedroom all these years.

Taylor picked it up. Now, her fingers stretched easily round the neck of the instrument. Yay! Progress!

Next Tay found a songbook and tried to work out how to twist her fingers into the right shapes to make chords. But her heart soon sank. It was just as hard as she remembered. On her CDs, the guitar made a clear, sweet sound. All she could produce was a tinny rattle that made her fingers hurt.

With a sigh, Taylor put the instrument back in the corner of her room.

But a few days later, everything changed.

There was a broken computer in the Swift house. Scott paced around, trying to work out how to fix it. Frustrated, he called the repair guy, Ronnie. Ronnie arrived that same afternoon. He knew exactly what was wrong, and the computer was soon running again. He was on his way out when he spotted Taylor's guitar leaning against the wall.

"You play guitar?" he asked her.

Taylor grimaced. "Not really. I want to, but..." She explained how hard she found it.

Ronnie nodded sympathetically. "It's not easy. But once you've got a few chords, you'll be away. Here, do you want me to teach you some?"

Taylor grinned. "That would be awesome! Thank you!"

Ronnie picked up the guitar. He showed her how to hold it so that her hand was at the right angle to grip the strings. "Now you try. Press these three strings with your first three fingers. That's right –

hold them down nice and firmly. That's a D chord."

Holding the chord with her left hand, Taylor began to strum with her right hand, up and down across the strings. It sounded so much better than before!

"Let's try an E chord," said Ronnie. "This one's a little harder. You need to stretch your hand a bit further over the neck to reach it. There!"

Ow! Holding E made Taylor's fingers hurt. But now the sound from the guitar was clean and pure. This was beginning to seem possible!

"How about A," suggested Ronnie. "Another easy one. Your first three fingers need to sit in a row – see?"

Once again, Taylor ran her fingers over the strings, sending notes trickling into the air. The sound of the chord was a happy one – matching the big grin on her face. Was it really as easy as this?

"There are a lot more chords to learn," Ronnie told her. "But three is all you need to write a song."

So the same evening, Taylor did just that. Ronnie was right. The three chords – A, E, D – fitted together perfectly. Within minutes, she had made a tune with them.

Now that she had decided to learn for real, Taylor put every ounce of her determination into mastering the guitar. She practised for four hours every day – six at weekends – starting with strumming and building up her range of chords, then moving on to fingerpicking.

Once she was confident on her six-string guitar, she started to play a twelve-string instrument. It was huge in her hands; her fingers could barely grip around the neck. But once Taylor had put her mind to it, there was no stopping her... despite the pain.

"Look at your hands!" exclaimed Scott as he caught sight of his daughter's fingers, cracked and bleeding from holding down the tough steel strings for hours on end.

Taylor wiggled her fingertips proudly.

"They'll soon be hard, like a proper guitarist's!"

Tay only had to imagine herself standing onstage with a guitar in her hands, playing to a crowd of thousands, to know the pain was worth it. Plus, she loved the feeling of getting better and better each day. The chords she had found hard last week? This week, they were easy. Practice really did make perfect!

While Taylor was busy perfecting her guitar skills, her singing skills were already in demand. Andrea had filmed her impromptu performance of the national anthem at the Phillies game, and her parents had sent the clip to stadium managers across Pennsylvania. With her crystal-clear voice, ringing with charm and sincerity, Taylor was a natural choice to sing the patriotic 'Star-Spangled Banner'.

The calls began to come. Almost every weekend for a year, Tay, her parents and brother Austin travelled across the state, and further, so Tay could sing at sports events. Once again, she realised how lucky she was. Taylor knew her parents would travel a million miles for her, if it helped her to achieve her dream.

The highlight came when Taylor was chosen to sing the national anthem for the Philadelphia 76ers. The 76ers were one of the best basketball teams in the country. Their stadium seated almost twenty thousand people. Standing at the edge of the court, under the glare of the floodlights, Taylor sang the familiar words to enthusiastic applause.

Then she spotted... was it really?

Yes! Sitting in the middle of the front row was the rapper Jay Z.

As Taylor left the court, the megastar singer reached out to high five her. A high five from Jay Z! Already she was mixing with music royalty!

CHAPTER 9

NEVER CHANGE WHO YOU ARE

There was just one thing in her life that Taylor would change if she could: school.

The feeling of being different that she had experienced when she first moved to Wyomissing four years ago had never left her. She had tried her best to fit in. Everyone else liked pop music, so she started listening to the Spice Girls, Natasha Bedingfield, Hanson, the Backstreet Boys and Britney Spears, alongside her country-music favourites.

But it wasn't enough.

The other kids were jealous of her parents' big house, their comfortable lifestyle and family holidays. They hated that Taylor was clever – she got good grades in all her subjects and her teachers were fond of her. Above all, they hated that she was beginning to make a name for herself locally, singing at big sports events and festivals. Taylor Swift seemed to have it all. The more successful she became, the worse the bullying got.

Surrounded by kids who taunted and teased her, thirteen-year-old Taylor had pretty much lost hope of being invited to parties. When she sat down in the cafeteria to eat her lunch, she knew it was likely that no one would sit down next to her. Sometimes the other kids would even move away when she approached.

But what Taylor dreaded the most was making the headlines. If an article about one of her performances appeared in the local paper, she knew the bullies would read it and make her life a misery at school the next day. She was so unhappy.

But Taylor kept on making an effort. She wanted to be accepted. Knowing her classmates liked shopping, one day she asked a small group of girls if they wanted to go to the mall with her.

"We can't," they told her. "We're busy. Sorry, Taylor."

Taylor sighed as the group walked away, giggling and linking arms. At least she had tried. Oh well – she would go with Andrea instead.

But when Taylor and her mum arrived at the mall later that afternoon, she spotted the same group of girls. Busy? They had lied to her!

"They didn't want to spend time with me," Taylor sobbed. "How am I ever going to make them like me, Mom?"

Andrea grabbed her car keys from her bag. "We're leaving," she announced. "We'll talk about it in the car, honey."

And they did. As they made the 45-minute drive south to the King of Prussia mall, Taylor told her mum everything that had happened that day. It was horrible to feel unwanted – but it was amazing to have a mum who would listen to her and support her, no matter what.

Arm in arm, they wandered around the shops, looking at jeans, dresses, shoes and bags. The bullies wouldn't go away, but Taylor knew that right now they didn't have any power over her. She could still have fun. She could still smile and laugh. The bullies had made her feel small and worthless, but her mum made her feel warm, cherished and special.

"I love you, Momma," Taylor told her. "I don't know what I'd do without you."

As for Andrea, she wished she could wave a magic wand, like in a fairy tale, and make things easy for Taylor. But she knew her daughter had to deal with this situation for herself – just as she would have to handle difficult situations throughout her life.

Taylor was strong. Andrea knew that eventually she would come out of this tougher and more sure of herself than ever.

"Don't give up, honey. Don't let their smallness make you feel small. Never change who you are to fit in."

Taylor held her mum's words close to her heart. She tried to focus on everything that was good about her life. And when the bullying got too much, well, she wrote it into songs, and that took away at least some of the pain.

In 2003 Taylor turned fourteen. With more gigs under her belt, more national anthems sung – and

Jay Z among her fans! – things were moving up a gear.

For the first time, Taylor had a manager: Dan Dymtrow, who was based in New York. Among his former clients was Britney Spears. Dan organised record company meetings. He approached Abercrombie & Fitch, who invited Tay to be a model in their 'Rising Stars' campaign. He arranged for one of Taylor's songs to be featured on a promotional CD published by Maybelline called *Chicks with Attitude*. He even got Taylor a part in a TV feature, *Nashville Dreams*, about aspiring musicians.

Most exciting of all, Dan organised for Taylor to take part in an RCA Records showcase in Nashville. Executives from all the major record labels would be there, scouting for new talent.

Taylor stood out. She had been right: there weren't many fourteen-year-olds who could play the guitar like she did.

"I have great news," Dan told her once the showcase was over. "Sony want to give you an artist development deal!"

He explained that the record label would

support Taylor to develop her music.

"You'll work with professional songwriters. Then, after a year or so, they'll decide whether to make an album with you. It's a great next step, Taylor."

Taylor and her parents agreed. And, hoping and praying for a different response, Taylor decided it was time to ask that question again...

"Mom, Dad, *now* can we move to Nashville?"

Scott and Andrea thought long and hard. Taylor's dedication had never been in question. Nor was her talent. They wanted to do everything they could to help her achieve her dream. But her eleven-year-old brother, Austin, was in middle school. Could they uproot him? And what about Scott's job?

Eventually they came to a decision. It was worth taking a chance. They believed in their daughter. They would move their family to Nashville, Tennessee – otherwise known as Music City!

CHAPTER 10

TIM MCGRAW

Outside, on the street, the lights of Music Row were glowing brightly, but hunched over her guitar on Liz Rose's songwriting sofa, Taylor's eyes had lost their usual sparkle.

"What's on your mind, Taylor?" asked Liz. She knew Taylor wouldn't need much prompting. The fourteen-year-old was quick to pour her heart out. "Is it the guy you told me about last week?"

For two hours every Tuesday evening, Taylor and Liz Rose wrote songs together. It felt to Taylor as though she was leading a double life: going to school like a normal teenager, then coming here to the studio to write with one of the best songwriters in Nashville. The only point where Taylor's two lives met was in the songs themselves. There she expressed her innermost thoughts, while taking a step closer to her dream of becoming a country singer.

Taylor groaned. "Brandon. Yeah. He's graduating this summer, and he's going to forget me. I know he is."

Taylor's boyfriend, Brandon, was seventeen, three years older than her. Liz frowned in sympathy. She had known Taylor for several months now, and she knew there was no point simply telling her that everything would be OK. Taylor never wanted false comfort. "That sucks, honey," she said.

"I know how to make it into a song though," Taylor said.

Liz smiled. She was never surprised to hear this. Taylor turned everything in her life into music. She reached for a notepad. Her job was to help Taylor say what she wanted to say.

"And the song is about a song," Taylor continued.

Liz looked puzzled. "What do you mean?"

Taylor explained. "I'm going to miss my boyfriend when he leaves. I'm hoping he'll think of me when he hears my favourite song."

"Ah!" Liz nodded, scribbling. "And what's your favourite song?"

"'Can't Tell Me Nothin'' by Tim McGraw." Taylor smiled, naming the famous country singer. "I hope Brandon thinks of me every time he hears Tim McGraw."

The glow had come back to Taylor's face. Writing always helped. Together she and Liz began to shape the song. Often Taylor's songs were written in less than half an hour. She had such a clear idea of what she wanted to say.

"And what are we going to call it?" asked Liz.

"'Tim McGraw'?" suggested Taylor. "Do you think he'd be pleased?"

School was a much happier place for Taylor now. She attended Hendersonville High School, and here Taylor's classmates were supportive of her musical ambitions. It such was a relief, after all those years of bullying, to have friends who didn't find her weird or annoying!

In English class, Taylor met her best friend, Abigail Anderson. The two girls clicked instantly.

Like Taylor, Abigail was ambitious. She wanted to be a professional swimmer. But Taylor's new friend didn't take herself too seriously either. The two of them joked around, while lots of the other kids acted too cool for school – literally. They also shared a love of music. Abigail was always listening to something new and interesting. And, of course, Taylor's best friend was also her most passionate supporter. She was the first person Taylor played all her new songs to.

With the help of Liz Rose, Taylor was rapidly building up a collection of memorable, heartfelt lyrics. She knew exactly how she wanted them to sound when they were recorded. In Tay's head, a country-music album was coming together. She felt ready to take the next step.

But her record label, Sony, didn't agree. She was too young, they told her. Perhaps in a few years' time she would be ready. They also wanted her to stop singing her own songs. Country-music fans wouldn't be interested in teenage problems, they said. Taylor needed to start singing about things that older fans cared about: work, marriage, family...

Taylor's heart sank. She wanted to sing about her own experiences, what she was feeling right now. She wanted to make music for teenagers like her. It had to be authentic!

So, with the support of Andrea and Scott, Taylor made a bold decision. She walked away from her development deal.

It was a big risk. Without the backing of a label, she might never make it as a singer. But what use was a record deal, if it wasn't on her terms?

Staying true to herself was more important than anything. Deep down, Taylor knew she had made the right choice.

CHAPTER 11

BIG MACHINE RECORDS

From the outside, the Bluebird Cafe didn't look like anything special. Tucked between a hair salon and a barber's shop, it appeared to be just another diner.

But it wasn't. To the people of Nashville, the Bluebird Cafe was legendary. For decades, the most talented singers and songwriters in the city had performed here. It was a place where country-music dreams came true.

Scott Borchetta had come here more times than he could count, but he never stopped feeling a thrill of excitement and anticipation every time he walked under the famous blue awning and into the dark interior beyond. The cafe was crowded this evening – as usual. The tables around the edges of the room were filling up quickly. The centre of the room was empty though. It was here that the performers would sing. Mics were waiting and the spotlights were already shining down, creating a warm glade of light to welcome the singers.

Scott made his way to a free seat and nodded politely at his neighbour. Around him, couples and groups of friends were chatting, but he knew they would stop when the music began. People didn't come here to talk. They came here to listen.

"It's a good line-up tonight," said Scott's neighbour, smiling. "Robert Ellis Orrall and Sharon Vaughn..."

Scott nodded. Robert and Sharon were talented singer-songwriters. He had heard both of them perform several times before.

"Then there's Aaron Brotherton..."

"Up and coming," said Scott.

"And a girl called Taylor Swift."

Scott shook his head. The name was new to him.

"Apparently she's a teenager," his neighbour added. "Fourteen."

Fourteen was very young for a country singer.

How mature could Taylor's voice be at just fourteen? And her songs? They certainly wouldn't have the depth of an experienced songwriter. "We'll see, I guess," said Scott. "Let's hope it's not a wasted evening."

His neighbour grinned knowingly. "Talent scouting, are you?"

Before Scott could answer, the singers appeared. With their guitars in their hands, they picked their way through the audience to the centre of the room. The crowd clapped, then fell silent as the opening chords of the first song filled the room.

It was usual at the Bluebird for the singers to perform together for part of the show, playing and singing each others' songs. Scott listened intently. All tonight's performers were strong. They were talented musicians, and their voices sounded great together. This was part of the magic of the Bluebird – it brought out the best in every singer.

But one performer in particular caught Scott's attention. He had expected fourteen-year-old Taylor Swift to be nervous, playing alongside more experienced singers. He had expected her to be eclipsed by their musicianship and vocals. But she wasn't. Taylor Swift had the ease and confidence of a musician twice her age.

Please, let her sing alone, he thought to himself.

And she did. The very next song was Taylor's, a solo. The room was quiet already, but this time, Scott had the feeling that everyone was holding their breath. He certainly was.

Taylor Swift's voice was clear and powerful. And her songs? They were teenage, yes, but her lyrics were heartfelt and truthful. They captured exactly what it felt like to be young and in love.

"She's got something," Scott's neighbour whispered.

Scott could only nod. His mind was made up. This girl was very special indeed.

Once the show was over, Scott hurried from his seat. He had to catch Taylor Swift. He had to speak to her. If only the room wasn't so crowded!

He finally found her, tucked away in a corner of the room, talking to a blonde woman. Her mother, perhaps?

"Taylor? Can we talk? My name's Scott

Borchetta. I'm a record executive."

Taylor's eyes grew wide and a huge smile lit up her face. "Thank you for coming!"

"That was an amazing performance you just gave," Scott continued. He turned to the blonde lady. "Wasn't it?"

The woman laughed. "She's pretty amazing, yes." She put out her hand and Scott shook it. "I'm Andrea, Taylor's mother."

Now Taylor spoke up. "I'm so glad you liked it, Mr..."

"Borchetta," said Scott. "Listen, Taylor. You've got huge talent. I'm looking for artists for my new label – and I want you to be my first signing."

Until recently, Scott explained, he had been an executive with Universal Records. But he was leaving Universal to set up a brand-new label, Big Machine Records.

"I want you to be part of it, Taylor, right from the beginning. I want to launch your first record. But I need to ask you to wait until Big Machine is up and running. Can you do that?"

Taylor and Andrea looked at each other. Scott

was offering them a record deal! But what if the new label didn't work out? Wouldn't Taylor be safer with a well-established company?

"Can I have some time to think about it?" Taylor asked.

"Of course. Let's talk in ten days' time," Scott suggested. "Call me."

It was a huge decision. The biggest of Taylor's life. But in the end, the choice was easy. Sony hadn't wanted a teenage artist. Scott Borchetta did – he believed in Taylor and the songs she was singing. And she believed in Scott and his exciting new label.

She rang Scott. Within minutes, it was agreed.

"I'm going to make a record!" Taylor whooped. "I'm actually making a record!"

CHAPTER 12

THE WAIT IS OVER

A few months later, Big Machine Records had a shiny new office on Music Row, its own staff and its very first signing: a talented singer-songwriter, just turned fifteen, hungry to launch her music career.

First though, Taylor and Scott Borchetta had work to do. Taylor had a huge stack of notebooks, full of songs. Many she'd written here in Nashville with Liz Rose, but some went back much further. She'd written many of her lyrics when she was a kid, lying on her bedroom floor. Out of these hundreds of songs, they needed to pick a selection of ten or so to make up an album.

The first song Taylor played Scott was 'Tim McGraw'.

Scott didn't hesitate. "I love it!" he told her. "That's your first single, right there." He explained that country-music fans would be intrigued by the title. "Everyone will ask themselves why Tim McGraw is in your song – and hopefully they'll buy it!"

Taylor beamed with delight. It meant so much that Scott loved her favourite song. What else should she play him? This was so hard! Every one of her songs had a special place in her heart.

Scott made the decision for her. "I want to hear *everything*."

Picking up her guitar, Taylor began to play. First there was 'Picture to Burn', a song full of rage about Jordan, an ex-boyfriend, and their break-up. Then there was 'Teardrops on My Guitar', a song about unrequited love. Her classmate Drew had no idea how much she liked him – and every day, when he told her about his new girlfriend, it made her feel like crying. Then there was 'Should've Said No'. Taylor had written this one out of anger at a boyfriend who had cheated on her. The words of the song were the same words she had said to him when she found out. There was also 'Our Song', which Taylor had written for a talent competition at school. Her classmates had loved it. And so did Scott.

"Not many teens can express what's inside them in the way you do, Taylor," he told her. "I know I couldn't when I was your age."

"I think I'd go crazy if I didn't write down what I'm feeling," Taylor explained. She was silent for a moment. "It would be amazing if my songs could help other kids to find a way of talking about stuff that's bothering them."

Scott nodded. "That's the best thing about music," he said. "It shows us that we're all in it together."

In addition to her songwriting talent, Scott was impressed by how hard Taylor worked. When she wasn't at school or working on new songs, she was online, building up her page on MySpace – a sort of early Facebook for music fans – where she released music clips, blogged about writing songs and playing gigs, and chatted with her followers.

"Keep on doing what you're doing," he told her.

"Building up a fan base is so important."

Soon Scott and Taylor had finished narrowing down her vast collection of songs to just a handful of the very, very best. The next step was to start recording.

Taylor picked debut producer Nathan Chapman to produce the album. Nathan had never made a professional record before. Scott was nervous about his lack of experience, but Taylor was determined. She and Nathan had been making demo recordings ever since she moved to Nashville. She knew how skilled he was. Eventually Scott agreed.

In Nathan's hands, Taylor's simple guitar recordings became something magical. He wove other instruments through the track: violins, bass, keyboard, percussion. He added punchy drum beats, pulsing with energy. Above all, though, he let her sparkling vocals soar.

The album, Scott and Taylor decided, would be called, simply, *Taylor Swift*. And the image on the cover? A picture of Taylor, her long, blonde curls cascading over her shoulders. Scott encouraged Tay to personalise the design. She drew flowers and butterflies, which the designer incorporated into the image. She also had fun placing hidden messages in the lyrics booklet, capitalising certain letters to spell out words or phrases: her secret inspirations for each song.

Suddenly it was all getting very real...

A few weeks later, in June, Taylor squealed with excitement as boxes and boxes of CDs arrived at the Big Machine office. Real, physical CDs – all with her face on the front!

But there was plenty of work still to do. There were only four months to go before the release date, and Scott wanted Taylor's record to be on the desk of every country radio DJ in the country. Radio play would be crucial in making the album a hit. Taylor and her mum helped to stuff hundreds of CDs into envelopes, ready to post, and Taylor whispered a secret message of good luck to each one that she packed: "Let this end up on the radio! Please!"

While Taylor's CDs were flying across America, arriving at radio studios large and small, her new manager was busy organising promotion. There would be television appearances as well as a massive radio tour. Taylor was going to be busy!

Finally, on 24 October, 2006, the wait was over. *Taylor Swift*, the album, was released to the world!

CHAPTER 13

COOKIE POWER

On the morning of the release of *Taylor Swift*, Taylor and Andrea woke up in a hotel room in New York. It was 4.30 a.m. Rubbing her eyes, Taylor rolled out of bed. It was still pitch-black outside the window, but she had somewhere important to be.

By 5 a.m., Taylor and her mum were in a cab, rolling through the surprisingly busy streets. It was true what they said about New York, thought Taylor. It really was the city that never slept!

By 5.30 a.m., they had arrived at the *Good Morning America* studio on Times Square. A cheerful assistant hurried them towards Hair and Make-up.

Eventually this would become a familiar routine for Taylor – but for now, it felt so weird. As she sat staring into a huge, brightly lit mirror, a make-up artist applied heavy TV make-up: thick foundation, blusher, sparkling eye shadow, mascara and glossy lipstick. So much make-up! Taylor hadn't even had breakfast yet!

The next hour went by in a daze. Wardrobe. Vocal warm-up. Meeting the host. Getting her bearings on set. Gobbling a breakfast muffin. Then, finally, an assistant knocked on the dressing room door: it was time to appear on live TV!

Perched on a stool, with her guitar across her knees, Taylor looked as confident as if she had done this a hundred times before. She answered the host's questions, then beamed as the live studio audience clapped her soulful performance of 'Tim McGraw'.

Within minutes, it was over.

"Well done, sweetheart," said Andrea. "I'm so proud of you."

Seconds later, Taylor's mobile rang. It was her dad, calling from Nashville. He and Austin had been watching the show at home.

"You were fantastic," he said. "You couldn't have done better. I love you, angel."

Phew! Her first live TV performance had been a success!

Taylor had plenty more opportunities to shine, in the months that followed. In addition to TV appearances, she and Andrea embarked on a huge radio tour, visiting studios all across the country to promote her album. Her secret weapon? Homemade cookies! The DJs couldn't resist them. With her bubbly personality, her catchy, heartfelt music and her delicious baked goods, Taylor Swift was winning new fans everywhere she went!

Suddenly offers of gigs were flooding in too. Tay was invited to open shows for the Rascal Flatts, Me and My Gang, George Strait and Brad Paisley. She said yes to everything, and soon found herself on the road, travelling around the USA with some of the biggest names in country music.

"I miss my own bed, Momma!" she joked to Andrea.

"Me too, honey." Her mother smiled. "Me too."

Andrea had been with Taylor every step of the way. Her daughter was still only fifteen. The two of them were spending more time on tour buses and in hotels than they were at home.

But it was worth it. Standing onstage in her lucky red cowboy boots, in front of a cheering crowd, singing songs she had written, was everything that Taylor had ever wanted. Amateur theatre, the Coffee Talk gigs, singing the national anthem, karaoke competitions... it had all been leading to this.

And there was more.

"You'll never guess what! Tim McGraw and Faith Hill have asked me to open for them on tour this summer," Taylor told Abigail on the phone one night. She was breathless with excitement.

"Seriously?" Abigail gasped. She knew Tim and Faith were two of Taylor's biggest heroes. "That's incredible, Tay! I wish you were here so I could give you a hug."

"Me too!" said Tay. The two girls missed each other so much, now that Taylor was away from school, on the road.

There was one big question though. What would Taylor choose to sing in front of real-life legend Tim McGraw?

"'Tim McGraw'," replied Taylor. "Obviously!"

"Obviously!" laughed Abigail.

By now, *Taylor Swift*, the album, had reached number five in the US charts. 'Our Song' had reached number one in the Hot Country Songs chart – making Taylor the youngest person ever to write and perform a number-one country song.

Tay had to keep on pinching herself. Was this really happening?

In mid-2007, at the CMT Awards in Nashville, Taylor won Breakthrough Video of the Year for 'Tim McGraw' and Female Video of the Year for 'Our Song'.

But the biggest excitement was yet to come.

"I can't believe I'm nominated for a Grammy!" squealed Taylor when she heard the news.

The Grammy nomination was for Best New Artist. Up against Taylor were Amy Winehouse, Feist, Paramore and Ledisi. The Grammys were the most prestigious awards in music. Taylor would be walking the red carpet with the world's greatest artists...

This was nothing short of epic.

On the night of the ceremony, Taylor wore a purple-satin prom dress, made specially for the occasion, with a trail of indigo leaves cascading down her skirt to the floor. She beamed for the cameras; everyone wanted a picture of the rising country-music star. She felt like a princess in a fairy tale.

Around her, Taylor spotted an endless list of celebrity singers, in beautiful gowns and immaculate tuxedos: Beyoncé, Jay Z, Kanye West, Mary J. Blige, Prince, Mariah Carey... and her original musical heroes, LeAnn Rimes and the Dixie Chicks.

In the end, the Grammy for Best New Artist was won by Amy Winehouse. But it didn't matter. Taylor had had the night of her life. Just to be nominated for this legendary award was the biggest honour she could imagine.

Could it get any better than this?

CHAPTER 14

FEARLESS

It was midnight on 10 November, 2008, and Taylor was at her local Walmart store in Hendersonville.

But she wasn't getting late-night groceries.

No – dressed in a simple white dress and brown cowboy boots, with her long, blonde curls tumbling down over her guitar – Taylor was performing. It was the night before the release of her second album, *Fearless.*

If sixteen-year-old Taylor had held any doubts about the passion of her fans, tonight they disappeared. The store was full of screaming fans who were calling her name and singing along to the songs they knew. At midnight, when the tills opened, they streamed through the checkouts, clutching their precious new albums and joining the huge queue for autographs.

With her guitar at her side, Taylor signed album after album, smiling and chatting to her young fans. This hadn't stopped feeling surreal... She, Taylor Swift, aged sixteen, had written and recorded the CD that she held in her hand! She had fans. People knew her name. They loved her music.

After an hour, Taylor's hand ached from writing her signature, and her mouth ached from smiling. But she didn't want to stop. She wanted to thank every single person who had come here to support her. It meant the world to her, and she wanted her fans to know that.

Despite their support, she hardly dared hope that the response to *Fearless* would be as amazing as it had been to her first album. Scott Borchetta had warned her: when a first album is a success, sometimes the second one isn't. The music industry can be fickle.

Taylor could only wait and hope. She knew her writing was getting stronger and stronger. She still wrote about her own experiences. Impossible crushes. Heartbreak. Friendship. Identity. She lived with her heart on her sleeve, and every day provided new inspiration.

There was one song that was particularly special to Taylor: 'The Best Day'. The previous Christmas, she had edited together clips from the Swifts' many home videos. She had found footage going right back to when she was a baby! The lyrics to the song described how her mum had always been at her side, loving and supporting her through the good times and the bad.

On Christmas Eve, as Andrea took a break from preparing the family celebrations, Taylor called her into the living room to play her the song.

"Sit down, Momma. I've got something I want you to hear."

On the TV, the video was playing. Andrea was speechless as she watched the montage of images of her daughter growing up. There, too, was her own smiling face – as a young mother, cuddling her infant daughter, taking her to the playground, giving Taylor her first pony ride... So many happy memories. Then there was the song... Her daughter's voice filled the room, singing words of love and tenderness.

"This is for you, Momma. To say thank you."

"Oh, Tay!" gasped Andrea. Tears were rolling uncontrollably down her cheeks. "My sweet, beautiful girl. You don't know how happy you've made me."

But Taylor did. She could see it in her mum's eyes, glistening with tears. She put her arms around the amazing mother who had held her through thick and thin. "It's because of you that I'm here, doing what I'm doing. I love you, Mom."

All Taylor could do now was wait and see if her fans would like it too.

If the response to Taylor's first album had been great, the response to *Fearless* was phenomenal. Taylor's fan base had been growing rapidly over the past two years, and her fans responded with delight to the new songs, written and sung from the heart.

The album debuted at number one in the US charts – a feat usually only achieved by the biggest names in pop. 'Fearless', 'Fifteen', 'White Horse',

95

'You Belong With Me' – Taylor's songs were playing non-stop on the radio. The DJs who had loved her first album jumped on the second. It didn't seem to matter that there were no homemade cookies this time!

And a bestselling album wasn't the only excitement...

Taylor's manager had been contacted by producers of hit TV series *Grey's Anatomy*, one of Taylor's favourite shows. Could they use 'White Horse' in the opening episode of season five? *Er... yes!* Watching the episode with her family, Taylor jumped around the room with delight. Right now, this minute, millions of people, all across the world, were watching her favourite show, hearing her song. It was the most extraordinary feeling.

And, the same month as *Fearless* came out, so too did a Taylor Swift doll. It had Taylor's long, blonde hair, a princess dress in powder blue and, best of all, Taylor's crystal-covered guitar, which she played during every gig.

Taylor and Abigail laughed over it.

"I'd have loved this as a kid!" Tay giggled. "Look,

she's even got her own little mic..."

"Keep this for your grandkids!" said Abigail.

"Oh I'm keeping everything," said Tay. As Scott Borchetta had told her, success could be fickle. This had been the craziest year – but who knew what the next year might bring?

She knew it could all disappear in an instant.

CHAPTER 15

T-PARTY

Taylor's success didn't disappear. The spark of Taylor Swift's fame was growing steadily into a blaze.

Two years went by in a crazy whirl of concerts, award ceremonies, TV appearances, recording studio sessions, parties... Everyone wanted a piece of the talented new country star, and Tay threw herself heart and soul into everything she did.

Finally Taylor turned nineteen. Along with Scott Borchetta and her parents, she decided that the time had come to go on her first headlining tour. It was the biggest, most exciting event in her career so far. She would travel across America, then on to Europe, East Asia and Australia.

Tay was dizzy with excitement at the idea of seeing the world. And there was no one that she'd rather see it with than Andrea, who would be travelling with her.

Amazingly, tickets to the 'Fearless' tour sold out within minutes. Taylor had been touring in America with other artists and bands since she was sixteen. She had often seen half-empty arenas, thousands of tickets unsold. But this... this was incredible!

"You deserve it," her dad told her. "You've worked so hard. I wish I could be there."

Scott Swift would be staying in Nashville with Austin. "We'll be thinking of you onstage each night," he told her.

A world tour was a huge project, but touring with other artists had shown Taylor what worked onstage and what didn't. She had spent hours sitting on tour buses dreaming of what she would do if she ever had a show of her own. The costumes! The special visual effects! The set! The dancing...

For months, Taylor had been meeting with video

and lighting teams, designers and set-makers. The 'Fearless' set was an epic creation, with stairs and towers onto which her lighting team would project images, changing the scene from a school library to a fairy-tale castle, at the flick of a switch. Taylor even wanted backstage to be special, a place for her performers to rest and relax. So she ordered lanterns, candles, oriental rugs, and covered the walls in pink, purple and gold fabrics. It felt like being in a beautiful tent in exotic Morocco!

The show opened on 23 April, 2009, in Evansville, Indiana. Backstage, Taylor paced through the candlelit green room, singing snatches from the opening song, 'You Belong With Me'. For three weeks, she and her musicians and backing dancers had been rehearsing in a warehouse in Nashville. Every note, every word, every move, every cue was etched on her brain. She grinned as her backing singers tumbled out of the dressing room, chattering and laughing. There was a party atmosphere backstage. Everyone was excited, ready to be out in front of tens of thousands of fans in the packed arena.

Taylor beckoned her band, her singers and dancers into a huddle.

"You're like brothers and sisters to me," she told them. "Thank you! This is going to be amazing. Let's go out there and be..."

"... fearless!" they all shouted.

It was time. Taylor led the way, up the steps, past the production crew, and onto an elevator platform that carried her up through the floor of the stage. Suddenly, as if by magic, she appeared onstage, a spotlight beaming down on her. In front of Taylor, the audience was in darkness. All she could see were thousands of glow sticks, blue and green, waving hypnotically like glowing sea creatures in an ocean of black. Her mind flashed back to singing the national anthem in packed stadiums. How surreal it had felt to hear her own voice filling the silence. But there wasn't silence now. Anything but...

"Taylor! Taylor! TAYLOR!"

The screams got louder and louder as her fans spotted her standing at the top of the set. This was what she had been dreaming of since she was eleven. A stadium audience of thousands was shouting for *her*!

"*TAYLOR! TAYLOR! TAYLOR!*"

For the opening song, 'You Belong With Me', Taylor was dressed as a band leader, in a white uniform with sparkling gold brocade. A white hat hid her long, blonde hair. The projections on the stage showed a locker room scene, and her dancers were dressed as cheerleaders and football players. Taylor had a story to tell: she was the uncool girl who couldn't get the cool guy she liked to notice her. He was only interested in the popular, pretty cheerleader. It was a tale she knew her young fans would understand.

The cheers were electrifying!

It was on... Dancing, playing her trademark crystal guitar, chatting to the audience, changing from one elaborate costume to the next, Taylor performed hit after hit: 'Teardrops on My Guitar', 'Our Song', 'Forever and Always', 'Fearless', 'Tell Me Why'.

Then came the coolest part of the show, the idea she was proudest of. Unfortunately, it was the only part of the performance she hadn't been able to practise.

Was this going to work?

With her tour manager at her side, Taylor left the stage and travelled via corridors and concourses to the back of the stadium. The tour manager checked his watch. Timed to perfection. Phew!

Onstage a video was playing – a spoof documentary showing Taylor's ex-boyfriends complaining about the songs she had written about them. Clutching her guitar, Taylor was tingling with excitement. As the video finished, she emerged at the back of the arena, between the rows of fans, lit by a spotlight as she began to sing 'Hey Stephen'.

These seats at the far end of the stadium had been the worst, the furthest from the stage – but suddenly they were the best in the house. The screams were ear-splitting as Taylor's audience realised she was behind them. The rest of the stadium watched on the jumbo screen as Taylor leaned across the seats to hug and kiss her fans.

"Taylor! Over here, Taylor! We love you, Taylor!"

From the opening note to the spectacular finale, the show had been a triumph. And there was one last thing that Taylor wanted to do for her fans. Before the show, she had sent her team into the audience to find the fans with the most imaginative outfits and invite them to her post-show 'T-Party'. Backstage in the Moroccan-themed tent, she organised drinks and snacks, a TV and sofas to relax on. Her fans went wild when the singer, her lucky '13' still painted in glitter on her hand, appeared in the doorway of the tent to hang out with them.

Doing things for her audience always felt good to Taylor. After all, her fans were the ones who allowed her to do what she loved. Chilling out with them was the perfect way to end this amazing show!

CHAPTER 16

GRAMMYS

Autumn had come round – and that meant awards season. There were new albums out from Beyoncé, Jay Z, Katy Perry and Lady Gaga. Did *Fearless*, a country album, have what it would take to go up against some of the biggest artists in the pop world?

Taylor's team was hopeful. The support for *Fearless* had been mind-blowing – greater than anyone could have imagined. This would be Taylor's year, they felt sure of it.

First up were the MTV Video Music Awards, where Taylor was nominated for the Best Female Video for 'You Belong With Me'. She was proud of her film. It was a rom-com movie in miniature, in which she played the girl who fancies the boy next door... who fancies someone else – a classic love story. Also nominated were videos from Beyoncé, Kelly Clarkson, Lady Gaga, Katy Perry and Pink.

Dressed in a glamorous gown of shimmering silver sequins, Taylor waited and hoped. At home, nine million people were watching on TV. Her dad and brother were among them, back home in Nashville. The tension was unbearable!

"And the award for Best Female Video goes to... Taylor Swift!"

Taylor's heart did a somersault. Surprised? She was flabbergasted!

Her stomach full of butterflies, Tay stepped onstage to collect her award from singer Shakira and actor Taylor Lautner. She pressed it to her chest, but as she opened her mouth to thank the fans who had voted for her—

Kanye West? What was he doing onstage?

Kanye bounded up to her. "I'm gonna let you finish," he said, "but Beyoncé had one of the best videos of all time!"

Taylor's mouth fell open. What?! Her eyes flew to the audience.

In her seat, Beyoncé looked shocked.

What was going on?

Kanye was booed offstage, but it was too late. Taylor had missed her opportunity to thank the fans she cared about so deeply. Suddenly, the awards evening – with all its glitz, glamour and excitement – tasted sour. Taylor deserved the award, she knew she did. How dare Kanye ruin her night!

Except that he hadn't.

Later that evening, it was Beyoncé's turn to shine, as winner of Video of the Year for 'Single Ladies (Put a Ring on It)'. She accepted her award, then invited Taylor up onto the stage.

"I'd like for Taylor to come out and have her moment!" said the megastar, to wild applause.

"Perhaps we can try this again!" joked Taylor. The crowd gave her a standing ovation and she finally delivered her speech, thanking her fans, her director, her video co-star – and her brother Austin's high school for letting them shoot the video there.

Beyoncé's generosity had saved the night. Taylor put Kanye from her mind and focused on celebrating her win. She wasn't the only one who deserved this award, after all – it was a team effort.

And who knew? One day, she might even write a song about this crazy evening!

Taylor's VMA was just the first of many, many awards for *Fearless*.

In November, at the BMI Country Awards in Nashville, she won three awards, including Country Song of the Year for 'Teardrops on My Guitar'. She had even convinced her camera-shy brother, Austin, to go with her to the ceremony. That was a victory of its own!

At the American Music Awards, Tay won Favourite Female Country Artist. This award was particularly precious to her, as it was fans who voted for the winner.

Then February 2009 came round, and it was time for the Grammys again. Taylor had eight nominations this time. But she hardly dared hope. Country-music awards were one thing. Surely she couldn't win a Grammy?

She was wrong.

Dressed in a midnight-blue sequinned gown,

Taylor was called to the stage to collect not one, not two, but four awards, including Album of the Year. She was the youngest ever winner of this massive award.

And the best thing? No interruptions!

"Back home, my dad and brother will be going nuts over this!" she cried, grinning at Andrea in the audience. "I hope you know what it means to me!"

And there was more...

Taylor won four gongs at the Country Music Awards, including Album of the Year and Entertainer of the Year. The awards were presented by two of her biggest country-music heroes, Tim McGraw and Faith Hill.

"I'd like to thank all the characters in my songs – Abigail, Tim McGraw... and Romeo," Taylor joked as she accepted the award. "If you've ever talked to me for more than five minutes, then I'm going to write a song about you."

It had been a truly momentous year. Taylor's success had exceeded every expectation – especially her own. Her career was offering up opportunities she could never have imagined in her wildest fantasies – plus a few she had been dreaming of since she was a child!

"Taylor, honey, come and listen to this. You won't believe it!" Andrea called from the study.

Taylor rushed in. "What is it, Momma? Is everything OK?"

"I've just been on the phone to the record company. You'll never guess." Andrea was grinning from ear to ear. "You've been offered a guest part on *CSI*!"

"Oh!" Taylor's squeal was ear-splitting.

She flew into Andrea's arms, jumping up and down with excitement. *CSI* was her all-time favourite series. Ever since she had first started watching it, she had dreamed of a role 'dying' on the show. Someone must have told the producers!

"This is crazy. Just crazy!" she cried. "I cannot believe my life sometimes. I have to call Abigail, right now!"

Andrea hugged her. "The part is a rebellious teenager. She's called Haley. Think you can play that?"

Taylor grinned. She had been the least rebellious

teenager she knew. At fourteen, when her classmates had been out partying, stealing alcohol from their parents, she had preferred to be at home, baking. But Taylor lived for a challenge. "It sounds like fun!" she said.

Taylor's *CSI* episode got an extraordinary twenty million viewers – and it was the first of several film and TV roles. Tay's theatre training was coming in handy!

First, she travelled to New York to appear on the sketch comedy show *Saturday Night Live*. Next there was a cameo appearance in *Hannah Montana*.

Then she was offered her first film role, in a rom-com, *Valentine's Day*, starring alongside Taylor Lautner and a host of major stars: Jessica Alba, Jamie Foxx, Anne Hathaway and Bradley Cooper. Taylor played a high-school student, Felicia, and Taylor Lautner played her new boyfriend, Willy. They filmed their scenes in a real school, during term time. Every half hour the bell rang and kids came streaming out of their classrooms – Taylor had forgotten how noisy and crazy high school was!

She had stopped attending Hendersonville High School at sixteen, as her touring schedule was too busy. Instead her parents had enrolled her in the home-schooling programme at Aaron Academy, where she intended to graduate with flying colours.

Tay and Tay had so much fun on set. Being in a movie was a new experience for Taylor Swift the singer. It was brilliant to have someone to show her the ropes. And there was something else too...

"I think I like him," Taylor told Abigail. "He's so cute and kind and funny. And he's an incredible kisser!" So far they had only kissed on set, but Tay couldn't help imagining what it would be like for real.

Abigail squealed. "You like him? Aw, Tay! Does he like you back?"

"I think so." Taylor giggled. "Yeah, I'm pretty sure he does."

"You should go for it!" said Abigail, smiling.

Taylor knew dating an A-list actor like Taylor wouldn't be easy. Her first celebrity boyfriend had been Joe Jonas, of the band the Jonas Brothers. She and Joe had been constantly on their guard –

the paparazzi loved nothing more than a celebrity couple. There had been cameras everywhere, waiting around every corner in the hope of photographing them holding hands or kissing.

But she *did* really like Taylor...

Tay grinned. She was excited to find out what it would like to be boyfriend and girlfriend for real.

CHAPTER 17

THE IMAGINARIUM

There were few opportunities to relax in Taylor's life these days. She was more likely to be starring in her favourite shows than sitting at home watching them, and everywhere she went, the cameras of the paparazzi were sure to follow. Taylor enjoyed the fun that fame had brought her – the premieres, the fancy hotels and glamorous parties – but she longed for quiet time, just hanging out on her own or with her family and closest friends.

The answer? An apartment of her own. Somewhere she could chill out and invite her friends. A place to truly call home.

Taylor was nineteen when she bought her first apartment in Nashville, a penthouse with a stunning view over glittering Music City below. Her new home was sleek and modern, styled in neutral whites and greys. But Tay had an imaginative new vision for it. She painted the walls bright colours and decorated the living-room ceiling with shimmering stars. She bought antique furniture and added mismatched handles – she loved shabby chic – and built an indoor pond, which she filled with koi carp. Finally, she installed a human-sized birdcage on the upper floor, with a large brass telescope inside it. Now she could look out across the whole of Nashville and up towards the twinkling night sky.

Tay called her apartment the 'Imaginarium': a place to think and dream and be herself – without the world watching.

Settled in her beautiful new home, enjoying her independence and her amazing view of the city, Taylor's creative juices were flowing. She found it almost impossible to spend more than a few days without writing a song. She always kept a notebook handy, no matter where she was – the star often had ideas at the most inconvenient times, like the second before she was about to go onstage!

And her material? Well, there was plenty of that. Taylor wore her heart on her sleeve. She fell in and out of love a lot!

Luckily, Taylor had amazing friends. There was Abigail, of course. Then there was Selena Gomez. They had met when Selena was dating Joe Jonas's brother, Nick. Selena understood the pressures of fame and especially how hard it was to be part of a celebrity couple. The two girls knew they could talk to each other about anything.

But Selena lived in Los Angeles, a five-hour plane ride from Nashville.

"I just wish you didn't live so far away, Tay," moaned Selena one day.

Taylor had flown from Nashville to spend the weekend with Selena in LA. The two friends were sprawled on the sofa in the beautiful house that Selena shared with her mum and stepdad. The table in front of them was strewn with crisp packets and chocolate bars. It could mean only one thing...

A break-up. Selena's, this time.

"I'm always here for you," said Taylor, throwing

her arms around her friend. "Wherever I am, Sel, I'll always come... and I'll always bring junk food. That's a promise."

Selena laughed. Just a few minutes ago she had been in tears, replaying her break-up with Justin Bieber. But Taylor always managed to cheer her up. She was like a funny, wise, caring big sister. With Taylor, Selena found it easy to say what was on her mind. It felt so good to be able to talk to someone who really got what she was feeling.

"And how about you, Tay?"

Taylor grimaced. Her love life had been complicated. She and Taylor Lautner had dated for three months. There was so much she liked about him, but...

"We split up a few weeks ago," Tay told her friend. She was sad about it, but he simply wasn't the right person for her. "I feel so bad, Sel. I think our break-up really hurt him."

"Poor Taylor – other Taylor." Selena smiled sympathetically. "Well, both Taylors," she added. Hurting someone else sometimes felt as bad as getting hurt. She knew her friend would never do anything to intentionally cause pain. "How are you feeling?"

"I'm so over boys," groaned Taylor. "Seriously, it's more hassle than it's worth... I'm done with dating."

Selena smiled. "You say that now, but..."

"I know, I know!" Taylor giggled. "You're right. I'm a romantic. I can't help it!"

"Me neither," said Selena. "Even if it means getting my heart broken sometimes."

They both knew it wouldn't be the last time they shared junk food while getting over a break-up. But maybe that was OK.

"We're teenagers," Taylor added. "This is what teenagers do. Date. Split up. Get over it with your friends."

Selena nodded. It was true. What they didn't understand was why anyone cared about their love lives.

"I'm really not that interesting," Taylor laughed, brandishing an empty crisp packet.

Selena grinned. "Me neither. I mean, just look at us!"

CHAPTER 18

SPEAK NOW

Back in Nashville, Taylor's next album was taking shape.

Channelling her experiences of friendship, romance, heartbreak and fame, she had written a brilliant collection of new songs. 'Back to December' was about her break-up with Taylor Lautner. She wanted to use the song to apologise for hurting him. 'Mean' was about someone who had hurt her: a music critic, who said such cruel things about everything she said and did. 'Innocent' was about the scene at the MTV Awards when Kanye West had run onstage and spoiled her time in the spotlight... Yes, she had finally written about that horrible night – she had always known she would!

Taylor was proud of her new music, and now she was back in the studio, working with her favourite producer, Nathan Chapman, to record it. The title she had chosen for the album was *Speak Now*. It felt amazing to be able to use her voice to speak about the things that mattered to her. She hoped her songs would help her young fans find their voices too.

Speak Now was released on 25 October, 2010. Once again, it debuted at number one. Taylor won three Grammys, including Best Country Album. Her performance of 'Mean' at the ceremony got a standing ovation.

A third hit album! Tay had triumphed again!

Next up, another tour. Taylor and her team had set the bar high with 'Fearless', but 'Speak Now' was going to be even bigger and even more spectacular. Over the course of a year, Taylor would play ninety-eight concerts in seventeen countries. A hundred and thirty people would work on the show, from musicians to technicians, carpenters to stage managers. Twenty-one trucks and thirteen buses would transport the tour from city to city. It was going to be epic.

The show began in February 2011. Just as Tay had planned, it was a stunning whirlwind of colour and fantasy, a magical journey into her wildest imagination. Onstage there was a giant bridge, a gazebo, a snowstorm, a fireworks display and a wedding scene – Taylor had insisted on the biggest meringue dress ever for the actress playing the bride! There was a tap dance solo from one of her amazing dancers. During 'Haunted', three acrobats tumbled from giant bells swinging above the stage. Then, in the finale – 'Love Song' – a flying balcony carried Taylor across the heads of her fans while back onstage, acrobats on ropes danced in midair and glittering confetti rained down on the audience.

The show was meticulously planned, of course, but Taylor also wanted to be spontaneous. Every night she performed a different surprise cover version from one of her favourite artists: Bruce Springsteen, Britney Spears, the Jackson Five, Eminem... She invited famous friends to duet with her too: Justin Bieber, who had supported her on the 'Fearless' tour, Nicki Minaj and Tim McGraw among them. On the final night of the tour's US leg, Taylor had an extra special surprise for her audience...

"On special occasions, you want to be surrounded by your friends," she said, standing on the ornate staircase in the centre of the stage. "And one of my best friends, she is such an amazing singer. In the four years we've been friends, we have never sung onstage together..."

A loud ripple of anticipation went through the crowd. Who would it be?

"It just so happens," Taylor continued, "that Selena is here tonight!"

The stadium erupted as Selena Gomez appeared at the top of the staircase. Together they sang Selena's hit 'Who Says'. On Taylor's left arm, she had written Selena's lyric 'You've every right to a beautiful life'.

It felt incredible to be sharing the stage with her best friend. And as for her fans – Taylor made them feel like every show was a party thrown especially for them.

CHAPTER 19

PAYING IT BACK

It was the night of 31 March, 2012. The event was the Nickelodeon Kids' Choice Awards. Onstage, a tall, elegant woman in a sequinned jacket was holding out a large silver statuette. The atmosphere in the room was almost reverential. The woman? Michelle Obama. The First Lady of the United States of America. With Michelle were her daughters, Malia and Sasha. They were here to present the Big Help Award to this year's winner.

"Taylor Swift may be in the news most often for her award-winning songs," Michelle told her audience, "but she's always made it a point to give back." She smiled warmly at the twenty-year-old singer. "She's supported children's charities. She's worked to combat bullying and given away over tens of thousands of books to schools and libraries."

Taylor's heart was thumping. Was this for real? She was standing in front of the First Lady, wife of the president – one of the most influential women in the country!

Michelle handed her the award, the silver KCA blimp, then reached to give Taylor a hug.

A hug from Michelle Obama!

Right now, Taylor Swift the megastar felt like Taylor Swift the ten-year-old schoolgirl.

"I'm freaking out," she told Michelle.

Taylor's award was well deserved. Her fans might know her best for her many small acts of kindness – she loved to make surprise visits to the homes of her most loyal Swifties and mail carefully chosen gifts to her fans at Christmas ('Swiftmas' as the Swifties called it) – but her generosity was on a much larger scale too. She gave millions of dollars to good causes and spoke in support of the work of many charities, including UNICEF and Oxfam. In May 2010, when Tennessee was hit by the worst floods in its history,

Taylor donated $500,000 to the clean-up operation. In 2008 she had given $100,000 to the victims of floods in Iowa. The previous spring, she had raised $750,000 for tornado victims in the southern states of America, by turning the dress rehearsal of the 'Speak Now' tour into a fundraiser. 'Speak Now... Help Now', she had called it.

Another cause close to Taylor's heart was literacy. When she was at school, she had won a national poetry competition with a rhyming poem called 'A Monster in My Closet'. If she hadn't become a singer, Taylor wondered if she might have become an author. So when she had the opportunity to become a reading advocate – after starring in *The Lorax*, based on Dr Seuss's famous story – she said yes at once. She and her co-star Zac Efron toured the country, speaking to hundreds of children about reading – and Taylor donated tens of thousands of books to schools and libraries.

Tay knew how lucky she was. Now she wanted to give something back.

The Big Help Award was just one of several accolades that Taylor received for her good work.

In 2011 she was named Billboard Woman of the Year for her contribution to the music industry and – the bit Taylor was proudest of – inspiring young women to achieve their potential in music.

Then, later in 2012, came a truly spectacular honour – one of the proudest moments of her life. She became the youngest ever recipient of the prestigious Ripple of Hope Award. The award recognised people who were helping to make the world a better place on a global scale. Past winners had included President Bill Clinton, Archbishop Desmond Tutu and George Clooney.

Taylor could hardly believe it. She was only doing her bit. But an honour like this? It was more than she could ever have dreamed of.

When she wasn't touring, winning awards and meeting the most famous women in the world, Taylor tried to spend as much time as she could with her friends. She had bought a new home in Beverly Hills, Los Angeles: a beautiful house with four bedrooms, a pool and a view of the Californian mountains. Being in LA, Taylor would be closer to many of her best friends, including Selena. She was excited to show her new home to her friend – and she had another surprise too.

"There's someone I'd like you to meet," announced Taylor as she welcomed her friend into her lavish new living room, decorated in her usual bright colours. "Selena, meet Dr Meredith Grey."

"Meredith Grey?" Selena was confused. She knew her friend loved *Grey's Anatomy* – had she invited its star? There was no one in the room. "What are you talking about, Tay? I can't see anyone."

Taylor grinned, then thrust a tiny ball of mewing grey and white fluff into Selena's hands. "*This* is Dr Meredith Grey. Isn't she beautiful?"

"You've got a kitten!" squealed Selena. "Oh, she's the cutest thing!"

It was true. With her big green eyes, her snow-white belly and silky grey tiger-stripes, Meredith was ridiculously cute.

"She's a Scottish fold cat. And before you say anything" – Taylor looked stern – "no, I'm not going to become a crazy cat lady."

Selena raised an eyebrow comically.

"OK, maybe a little bit!" Taylor laughed. "But in a good way."

Taylor took her tiny pet back and snuggled the kitten against her cheek. "Meredith is so chilled," she said. "Literally nothing freaks her out. I think she could even come on tour with me."

Selena could imagine it instantly: Taylor cuddling her cat backstage, minutes before stepping out in front of a crowd of tens of thousands. She laughed. "But won't she destroy the tour bus?" She knew how proud Taylor was of her lavishly decorated bus. She had bought it from the singer Cher and redesigned the interior in her unique style. An energetic young cat would rip it to shreds!

Taylor shook her head. "Dr Meredith is very well behaved. She's a credit to cats everywhere."

CHAPTER 20

RED

Of course, hard-working Taylor had already begun to write songs for her next album, her fourth. Writing songs was like breathing to her. She couldn't live without it. There was always something she needed to write about – the highs and lows of fame, friends, boyfriends, break-ups. Particularly break-ups!

This time round, Taylor was collaborating with Swedish songwriter-producers Max Martin and Karl Johan Schuster (who was known in the music industry as Shellback). Tay had made three country albums, but now she wanted to record something different. She wanted to sound like a pop artist. Max and Johan had worked with Adele, One

Direction, Pink, Britney... the list went on and on. If anyone could help her, they could.

Taylor, Max and Johan were hard at work in the studio one afternoon, experimenting with instrumentals at the sound desk, when a call came through from the reception. Someone was here to see Taylor.

"Let's take a break," she said. At home or in the studio, Taylor always loved to have visitors. She grabbed her coffee. "See you back here in ten?"

But when Taylor returned a few minutes later, she was in tears. Tears of rage.

"Taylor! What's going on?" asked Johan.

Her voice cracking with anger, Taylor explained. "That was a friend of Jake's."

Max and Johan knew she was talking about Jake Gyllenhaal, the actor and her ex-boyfriend. Tay and Jake had had a whirlwind romance – under the close gaze of the paparazzi, of course.

"His friend told me she had heard we were getting back together," Taylor continued.

Max was puzzled. "Ah, so you're back with J—"

"We're not!" Taylor snapped. "But why would

she say that? What did he tell her?" She was fuming. "We are never *ever* getting back together!"

There was silence for an instant. Max and Johan looked at each other. Each knew what the other was thinking.

In another second, Taylor knew it too. "This is a song," she exclaimed. "I need to write about it."

Max nodded. "That line – *we are never ever getting back together* – it's simple and powerful."

Taylor sang it, like she often sang her thoughts. She channelled all the anger and powerlessness she felt into her words, strumming her guitar as she sang.

"You don't think it's too... obvious?" she asked nervously.

"It's direct – that's what's so great about it," said Max. "Why make it more complicated than it needs to be? Sing like you're talking to him."

Taylor took a breath. Her heart was pumping. She could feel a warm flush on her cheeks. It was partly anger – and partly excitement. An idea was brewing in her mind. "That line I'm singing isn't clever or funny," she said slowly. "It sounds a bit teenage and tantrum-y. He'd think it was completely uncool."

She was grinning now. Max and Johan looked at each other in confusion. Just minutes ago, Taylor had been brimming with rage.

"He thinks he's so sophisticated," Taylor explained. "He's always talking about obscure indie bands that no one's ever heard of. Whereas this – this will be a super-simple catchy pop tune, nothing more. I can't believe I didn't think of it before! It's a sort of... musical revenge!"

Max laughed. "Let's do it then. Let's make your super catchy, not-at-all-sophisticated break-up song!"

So they did. In half an hour, the basics of the track were recorded. It didn't have Taylor's usual country-music vibe. It was a pop song through and through.

"This is gold!" said Max.

Johan nodded. "It's the kind of song that goes round and round in your head for days."

Already Taylor could imagine herself performing it onstage. She could hear it filling a vast arena. It was a tune that would get a whole stadium onto its feet, stamping and cheering.

"We are never ever getting back together." Taylor spoke the line again. How good it sounded. "That's the title of the song. Perfect."

Tay had a feeling it might just be her biggest hit so far.

And the red-hot rage she had felt had also given her an idea for the title of the album...

Red sold a phenomenal 1.2 million copies in the US in its first week. At just 22, Taylor had made the fastest-selling album of any artist in over a decade – and her third number-one album.

The fans clearly loved *Red*. And so did the critics. Taylor just couldn't seem to stop winning awards...

She was named Favourite Country Artist at the Peoples' Choice Awards. Tay hadn't totally shaken off her country roots!

She won four awards from the American Music Association: Artist of the Year, Favourite Female Country Artist, Favourite Female Pop Artist and Album of the Year.

She won a Grammy for 'Safe and Sound', which

she had written for the *Hunger Games* soundtrack.

It seemed that everything Taylor touched – even *Red* – turned to gold!

Theming her next tour around the colour red was a no-brainer. Taylor wove it through the visuals from the start to the finish: her red crystal guitar, her red-satin evening gown, her bright red lipstick. She kept the other colours of the show simple – black and white – and decided to keep the staging simple and intimate too. With her amazing backing singers, talented dancers and brilliant choreography, Taylor knew she had what it took to hold the audience's attention without complicated scene-setting and special effects.

It was only during 'We Are Never Ever Getting Back Together' that Taylor unleashed the dazzling spectacle that her fans knew her best for. Her own character was a circus ringmaster, dressed in a sparkling tailcoat – red, of course. She strode around the stage, summoning clowns, stilt-walkers, dancing dolls, and even a magician's white rabbit.

And the crowd sung along with wild, foot-stamping joy. It was just as she had imagined it, that day when she recorded the song with Max and Johan – the perfect finale!

Being on tour often was lonely for Taylor. She missed her friends and family. Usually she would spend hours on FaceTime, catching up with their news. She hated feeling so distant.

But this time, it was different. Taylor had brought one of her best friends on tour with her. Ed Sheeran had sung with Tay on 'Everything Has Changed' and now he was her support act for the US leg of the tour. It felt so good to have a friend around to share the highs and lows of life on the road. There was nothing she and Ed couldn't laugh about.

"When are people going to stop asking if we're an item?" joked Ed one evening. "I mean, I'm flattered, obviously, but..."

Ever since Taylor had dated Harry Styles, earlier that year, the media were more obsessed than ever with her love life. 'Haylor' had only lasted a few months – and now reporters tried to turn any man Tay talked to into her next boyfriend.

"I guess I need to tell them the truth," Taylor

joked back. "Which is that I only asked you on tour because you've got red hair. Come on, this is the 'Red' tour."

Ed pretended to look offended. "I'm going to dye it then. Or wear a wig. Green. No, purple. Wait – stripy."

"If you do that," giggled Taylor, "I'll make you perform on a trampoline tomorrow night."

Now it was Ed's turn to snort with laughter. Taylor had a trampoline in the garden of her home in Nashville. They had written 'Everything Has Changed' while bouncing on it. "Well," said Ed, "we already know I can bounce and play guitar at the same time, so..."

The memory made them both smile. Surely it was the weirdest place anyone had ever written a song!

Taylor's shows were changing. Her sound was changing. But one thing never did. She still loved to connect with her fans.

Seven-year-old Grace had been on her way to see the show in Columbia when she was hit by a speeding car outside the stadium. Her skull had been fractured in several places. Grace survived – but, of course, she missed seeing her hero onstage. When Taylor heard of the accident, she wanted to do something special for her young fan. So when Grace finally got tickets to see the show at another venue, Taylor surprised her with an invitation to come backstage.

"I've got a cold," Taylor told her VIP guest. "Will you sing extra loud to help me out?"

Yes, Grace would! She knew every word of Taylor's songs by heart.

"I was eight when I went my to first concert," Taylor told her. "I saw LeAnn Rimes. I loved it so much. If I'd missed it, who knows? Maybe I would never have become a singer. I'm glad you've come to see my show, Grace. Thank you!"

Then she autographed the sleeve of Grace's T-shirt with the words *I heart Grace! Taylor*.

Grace let out a squeal of delight. What she was feeling right now, being hugged by her idol, there were no words to describe it!

"That T-shirt will never go in the wash!" laughed Grace's mum.

CHAPTER 21

FOURTH OF JULY

Taylor had always loved the Fourth of July, American Independence Day. Back when her family had spent the summer in Stone Harbor, the celebrations had always been the highlight of the holiday. She loved to see the whole town decorated with the American flag, the Stars and Stripes. She and Austin watched the boat parade with their friends and threw water balloons at the yachts. This year, she wanted to recreate all the fun of childhood summers with her best friends, her Squad.

While Taylor's apartments in Los Angeles and Nashville were her havens to relax in, her new home in Rhode Island, on the East Coast, was her playground. The house overlooked the bay and she loved to wake up on a summer morning with a view of the vast sky and blue sea stretching into the distance. The mansion had a huge pool, acres of lawn and a high wall that kept her safe from the prying eyes of the paparazzi.

She wanted to host a party of epic proportions!

But first things first...

"Invitations," Taylor said to Meredith, who was curled on her lap. On the other side of the room, Olivia Benson, Taylor's second cat, a member of her feline family since 2014, was perched on a bookcase, chewing one of Taylor's MTV awards. "Stop that, Olivia! Leave my moonman alone. We need to focus. We need a list."

Taylor's new house was enormous. There was no limit to the number of friends she could invite. And Taylor had plenty of friends.

"OK, Meredith. I'm glad one of you is helping me. Now, who shall we ask? Selena. Ed. Cara..."

Selena Gomez. Ed Sheeran. Cara Delevingne, who had appeared onstage with her in London as part of her '1989' tour.

"Karlie, naturally."

Taylor's walls were covered in photos of her road trip along the Californian coast with Karlie Kloss, the model. Her friend loved adventure *and* baking – they were a match made in heaven.

"Blake and Ryan."

Blake Lively and Ryan Reynolds, the actors.

Taylor stopped to tickle Meredith, who had rolled onto her back, waving her white paws in the air. "Do you have anyone you want to invite, Meredith?"

Meredith purred loudly.

"No, I didn't think so. Oh – Abigail, of course!"

No party would be complete without Taylor's childhood best friend. Abigail loved a party, and—

"Listen, Meredith! I've just had a wonderful idea. I'm going to buy a slip-and-slide. Abigail will love that!" Her best friend was a swimmer – and this would be the pool party to end all pool parties!

Meredith looked unimpressed, while up on the bookcase, Olivia Benson took no notice of her megastar owner and was still attacking the silver statuette.

"Olivia, be careful!" called Taylor as the award tottered closer and closer to the edge of the shelf. "I have to work hard for those, you know."

July was still a long way away, but already Taylor was buzzing with excitement, her mind full of summer sunshine, friends – and baking. There would be plenty of cake!

"I throw a pretty good party, don't I?" Taylor said to Meredith. "Ooh – another idea. Matching swimsuits. What do you think?"

Meredith responded with a loud purr, while Taylor's statuette finally tumbled from the shelf and hit the floor with a crash.

"Oh, Olivia... how many times?!"

In the end, Taylor's party was more of a festival, lasting all weekend. The Squad swam in the sea, tumbled down the water slide, ate burgers, fries and homemade cookies, then watched a glittering fireworks display as night fell over the bay. Taylor giggled to see her friends wearing the matching red, white and blue swimsuits she had ordered – along with fluffy Stars and Stripes towelling robes.

"We could not look more patriotic right now," she laughed. "We have to get a picture!" Her friends bundled into a tight huddle and Taylor stretched her arm out to take a selfie. "That's definitely one for Instagram."

Surrounded by her best friends, old and new, Taylor felt so happy. Friendship meant everything in the world to her. How lucky she was to have these wonderful people in her life!

CHAPTER 22

BITING BACK

"I had the weirdest dream last night."

Taylor was in the studio with Max and Johan, working on a new album. The two men smiled at each other – it wasn't the first time Taylor had told them about her dreams. It was bound to be something strange!

"I woke up in the middle of the night with this rhythm in my head. Listen – and don't laugh!"

Taylor played them the voice memo she had made during the night. She was singing a high-pitched, energetic tune – *"Duhnuhunuhunuh"* – followed by a pause and a deep, almost growly sound – *"De-de-de-de-de-de-duh"*.

"That's what I could hear in my mind," said

Taylor. "You remember that song I was working on yesterday, on the piano?"

"'I Did Something Bad'? Yes, of course," said Max. "It's coming together nicely."

"It needs something else though. And I think my recording is the chorus."

Taylor often worked like this. Small fragments of a song would come to her at the strangest times. In the shower. On the tour bus. Before going onstage. And now, in her dreams!

"Can you recreate it?" asked Taylor. "The first part, 'duhnuh', should be me singing. But I want the second bit, the deep bit, to be an instrument."

Max shook his head. "There's no instrument that will make that sound, Tay."

Oh. It wasn't often that Max said no. But if *he* couldn't do it, no one could. She would have to rethink...

"I have an idea though," Max continued. "Sing it to me again."

"*De-de-de-de-de-de-duh*," sang Taylor. She was giggling now. "*De-de-de-de-de-de-duh*."

Sitting in front of the computer, Max applied

distortions. He lowered the sound of Taylor's voice electronically until it sounded like a man's deep, bass voice.

"That's it!" shrieked Taylor. "That's the sound. Max, you're a genius!"

Max fed in a drum beat, and suddenly 'I Did Something Bad' came to life.

"Amazing! That's perfect!" Taylor cried.

Tay loved the production process – hearing the simple tunes that she composed on the guitar or piano becoming proper pop songs, with rich instrumental lines and powerful beats. Already she was thinking about the staging: the lighting, the costumes, the special effects. She could see herself performing 'I Did Something Bad' onstage: there would be fireworks going off behind her, white strobe lighting slicing through the stadium like a knife...

This album was the third time Taylor had collaborated with Max and Johan. *Red* had been a massive hit. *1989*, released two years later, had been even bigger, winning Taylor a Grammy for Album of the Year. By now, Taylor had well and truly cast off her country-music label. She was a pop star through and through. No – a pop megastar.

Tay had been thinking for weeks about possible themes for this new album, her sixth. The songs she was drawn to the most were about fame. Taylor had many friends, but the last few years had taught her an important, and difficult, lesson: not everyone wanted to see her succeed. She thought back to that evening at the Grammys when Kanye West had jumped onstage and tried to ruin her celebration. Being famous sometimes felt like being back at school, surrounded by bullies who were always trying to knock her down, no matter what she did.

And then there was her love life. Taylor had dated some of the most famous actors and singers in the world: Joe Jonas, Taylor Lautner, Jake Gyllenhaal, John Mayer, Harry Styles, Tom Hiddleston. Her life was always in the spotlight, always being talked about. But the things that people said weren't always true – she was an easy target for hurtful gossip and cruel rumours.

Tay had been called a liar, a snake, and worse. It sometimes felt like other people in the industry were trying to destroy her reputation.

It was hard to know who to trust.

But Taylor knew her strength was in her music. No one could take that away. With the help of Max, Johan and a talented producer called Jack Antonoff, a collection of amazing songs was coming together: 'I Did Something Bad', 'Look What You Made Me Do', 'Delicate', 'End Game'... Through these new songs, Taylor felt bolder and more confident than she had ever done. This music had power. It had aggression. It had bite.

I'm biting back, thought Taylor.

An idea was forming itself in her mind – a theme for her album. A new direction.

"Reputation," said Taylor. "That's it. These songs are about the people who have tried to destroy my reputation. That's the name of the album... *Reputation.*"

A kaleidoscope of thoughts was whirling around her brain. Tunes, images and words were flashing in front of her eyes like a video montage.

Scenes from her past – the endless stream clips on YouTube showing her triumphs and humiliations, the Kanye moment, paparazzi photos of her kissing ex-boyfriends – then images of a new, stronger, more powerful Taylor.

The old Taylor. The new Taylor.

But there was one image in particular that kept recurring in her mind, slithering into all her thoughts, coiling itself in a corner of her brain, waiting...

CHAPTER 23

REPUTATION

It was 21 August, 2017. It was time. Taylor opened her Instagram and chose a video from her gallery.

Filter.

New post.

Share.

Her eyes locked onto the view count. *One. Five. 186. 698. 1K. 6K...* The number was shooting up quicker than her eyes could follow. Within seconds, thousands of fans had watched her video: a dark, grainy image of a slithering, scaly creature. Some kind of reptile? A lizard? Questions began to stream in. What did it mean? Was a new album coming?

Taylor smiled. Her fans would have to wait.

The next day, the mystery deepened as Taylor

shared a second video. It flickered like an old-fashioned VHS recording, and seemed to show the body of a serpent, its scales glinting in the poor light. By now, millions had watched the two videos.

On 23 August Taylor shared the final video. Like the first two, it was only a few seconds long. This time, a ridged head shot forwards and two unblinking orange eyes stared at the camera. Then the creature's mouth flashed open, revealing a set of deadly fangs and a flickering, forked tongue.

A snake! Taylor had been called a snake – and she had taken her revenge in the most powerful way. She had claimed the snake as her own!

A day later, her excited fans discovered what the grainy reptile meant: the singer's new single, 'Look What You Made Me Do', was out.

What a song! And what a video...

Taylor's imagination had conjured a fantasy that was darker and more lavish than anything she had ever created before. There was zombie Taylor, crawling out of her own grave. Diva Taylor lying in a bathtub of diamonds. Regal Taylor drinking tea on a golden throne. Finally there was a pile of old Taylors, fighting and bickering while the new Taylor towered goddess-like above them.

The old Taylor was dead. The new Taylor had risen to take her place.

And crawling, slithering, writhing through the whole video were snakes.

The fans went wild. The video clocked an astonishing 43.2 million views during its first 24 hours on YouTube, easily breaking the previous record for the most-viewed music video in a day.

The countdown to *Reputation* had begun.

Three months later, in November 2017, came the release everyone had been waiting for. *Reputation* the album was out.

The cover showed Taylor in black and white, against a background of newspaper headlines. Taylor had also created two magazines to accompany the CD. Inside were personal photos, fashion photography, handwritten lyrics, poetry and paintings by Taylor. Why give interviews to the media and go to fashion shoots when she could create them herself?!

And Taylor hadn't forgotten her famous sidekicks, Meredith and Olivia. Photos of her beloved cats featured in both magazines.

Reputation sold two million copies in its first week.

Taylor won the American Music Award for Favourite Pop/Rock Album and the Billboard Music Award for Top Selling Album. By now there was barely enough shelf space in her four houses to display all the awards she had won – but Taylor never stopped feeling amazed. Walking the red carpet still made her heart thump like it had when she was sixteen.

What Taylor was most looking forward to, though, was taking her big, bold, snake-filled show on the road. By now, she was the queen of the stadium tour. Sparkle? Spectacle? Drama? Taylor was planning to deliver it all.

After months of hard work with set designers, costume makers and lighting technicians, her latest tour was ready. The colours, costumes and lavish special effects Taylor had been dreaming of since she wrote the very first songs for this album were now a reality. And of course there was her cast of talented singers and dancers, who would bring the show to life each night. Everything was set for a truly unforgettable gig.

And there was one part of the performance that Taylor knew her audience would be waiting for – 'Look What You Made Me Do'. Giant screens filled with images of Taylor, past and present: polaroids, clips from TV and online media. Her dancers filled the famous tilted stage that she 'hated' in the lyrics.

And then came the snakes.

On the jumbo screen, a huge animated serpent lashed out at Taylor and her band. At the side of the stage, a vast inflatable cobra loomed menacingly. From that instant, the snakes were everywhere, writhing around on-screen, on the set, on the fingers of her dancers... During 'Shake It Off', two luminous technicolour snakes, with flickering tongues, rose up from the audience. Then Taylor hovered over her audience inside a metal snake with flashing red eyes to sing 'Bad Blood'.

In addition to her many special guests – Selena Gomez, Robbie Williams and Shawn Mendes among them – Taylor played a different, surprise acoustic song each night. By the time the tour ended, she had sung almost every song she had written and recorded, going right back to her very first album. Taylor knew her fans cared about all her songs. They had come on this journey together.

"I love how much you care about the lyrics. I love how much you care about human emotion," she told her audience. "I've been doing this since I was sixteen. I'm twenty-eight now. You guys have gone through a lot of things that I've gotten to see."

It was true. Taylor followed the lives of many of her fans over Instagram and Tumblr. She found their stories inspiring. One fan had listened to Taylor's music while she found the courage to come out to her parents. Another fan had supported her mother through a life-saving operation. A third had struggled with bullying in high school – Taylor knew that feeling well.

"And," Taylor added, "I've gone through a lot of things you've gotten to see. I love seeing the phases of our lives and going through them together."

For the finale, styled like a massive house party,

Taylor and her band performed a medley of 'We Are Never Ever Getting Back Together' and 'This Is Why We Can't Have Nice Things'. Fireworks – white, green, pink, red – lit up the skies above the stadium, while onstage, Taylor's dancers whirled around a marble fountain that sent plumes of water up into the air in perfect time with the music.

By the end of the run, over two million people had seen the 'Reputation' tour – another world record for Taylor. And one show was particularly special – in Nashville, Tay's musical home, Abigail and Karlie were in the audience. Instagram was soon buzzing with their pictures and comments, full of pride for their friend. Karlie said it best: *No one puts on a show like Taylor Swift!*

TAYLOR SWIFT

CHAPTER 24

JINGLE BALL

December was always Taylor's favourite time of year. First there was her birthday on 13 December. Then there was the fun-filled run-up to Christmas. Parties! Shopping for presents! Carol singing! Whichever city she was in, Taylor loved to see the streets hung with festive lights and shop-window displays sparkling with red, gold and green, while Christmas music spilled out from every doorway. Most of all, she loved the Christmas trees, with their glittering decorations. Real ones were the best – the magical smell of fir trees took Tay back to being a child, growing up with her family on the Christmas-tree farm.

"Do you remember that year I ruined Christmas?"

Taylor asked Andrea, giggling.

Tay and her mum were backstage in Taylor's dressing room at The Forum in Los Angeles. In a few hours' time, she would take to the stage to sing songs from *Reputation* at the annual Jingle Ball.

"Oh, Taylor," Andrea laughed. "How could I forget?!"

As a child, Taylor's most important job on the farm had been to pick praying mantis eggs off the trunks of the Christmas trees before they were cut down and sold. The clusters of eggs looked like walnuts, and young Taylor was expert at find them.

"Then that one year, I forgot," Taylor said. "People bought trees with eggs on them, and they hatched as soon as they got inside, into the warm..."

The homes of West Reading had been overrun with baby praying mantises... The little insects were harmless, but—

"It freaked people out so badly!" Taylor squealed, clapping a hand to her mouth. "I gave everyone a really bad Christmas that year. But I never forgot to check the trees after that!"

Andrea dissolved into laughter. "We had fun on the farm, didn't we?"

Taylor nodded. She couldn't have imagined a better childhood. "Remember when I first went to school, and the other kids laughed at me for having such messy hair from always running about the farm?"

"And rolling around in the hayloft," added Andrea.

Taylor glanced around her, grinning at the sight of all the styling products, tongs and wands laid out on the dressing table. "No risk of messy hair now!" she laughed.

In fact, Taylor had a whole team to take care of her hair, make-up and clothing. Tay spun round to smile at them. With just two hours till the show, it was time to get ready.

"Work your magic!" she said.

Taylor's hairstylist tamed her naturally curly hair into smooth waves. Her make-up artist carefully applied glittering eyeshadow, mascara and Tay's trademark red lipstick. Then her stylist brought out a golden sequinned snakeskin top and black shorts.

Perfect! Taylor slipped her feet into black boots with golden snakes wound around them.

She was ready.

"You're beautiful, honey," said her mum. "Inside and out. I'm so proud of you. Have fun out there."

"Always!" laughed Taylor.

In the vast auditorium, sitting in her VIP seat, Andrea watched as her daughter performed the hit songs from *Reputation*. Taylor must have sung them a thousand times by now. Even Andrea had heard them hundreds of times. But with each performance, it was as if it was the first time. They sounded so fresh, so exciting.

Andrea felt a lump in her throat as she thought back to watching her teenage daughter performing at country-music festivals, wearing her favourite cowboy boots, with her crystal guitar slung over her shoulder, just a few hundred people in the audience. How far she had come... The Taylor she was watching now was a ten-time Grammy winner. She was pop royalty, playing 100,000-seater stadiums. Andrea shook her head in disbelief. It simply didn't seem real sometimes!

Onstage, Taylor was talking to her audience.

"If you cheer loud enough," she encouraged them, "there's a chance someone might come out..."

And he did.

As cheers erupted from the crowd, Ed Sheeran appeared beside Taylor, like a genie from the bottle. The two friends flung their arms around each other, then sang their duet, 'End Game'.

Taylor knew how lucky she was. In the audience was her amazing mum, who had been with her for every step of her musical journey. At home, she knew her dad would be watching the show on TV. Without her parents, none of this would have been possible. She looked at Ed, beside her. Without her closest friends, Abigail, Selena, Ed – all the incredible people who had been with her through thick and thin – she would never have come this far. Cruel critics? Angry exes? None them mattered, when Tay had friends like these.

And that just left her fans.

Looking out at the glittering sea of phones, glow sticks and waving arms, Taylor felt a rush of love for her loyal Swifties. They were the reason she was on this stage, right here, right now, holding a mic in her hand. Her fans amazed and surprised and inspired her every single day – and hearing them singing along to her songs was simply the best feeling in the world. Nothing would ever change that.

Tay hit the final note and raised her microphone high into the air, listening to the screams and the cheers of this happy, excited crowd. She would hug every single one of them if she could.

"Merry Christmas, everyone!" she shouted. "I love you! Let's do this again sometime!"

Turn the page for a sneak preview of another
inspiring *Ultimate Superstars* story...

SELENA GOMEZ

Available now!

978-1-78741-521-8

CHAPTER 1

CHANGING THE GAME

"I'm telling you to trust yourselves – always."

Selena Gomez crossed the stage to touch the hands of her fans in the front row. As she did, hundreds of hands reached up to grab hers. Tucked under her right arm was a piece of paper, her speech. But she didn't use it. She didn't need to. Selena knew exactly what she wanted to say to her audience at WE Day, California.

She told them that she had always dreamed of being an actress, but how, aged eleven, a casting director had told her she wasn't good enough.

"I'm sure all of you have been told that you're not good enough. It crushes you. And it almost did for me..."

It hardly seemed possible. Selena Gomez – the singing star and actor, with over 100 million followers on social media – *not good enough*? Surely everyone had always told her how amazing she was?

"But there was my mom, next to me," explained Selena, "and she said that the most important thing was to always *trust in myself*. She told me to keep going. If I didn't believe I could do it, I wouldn't be here."

The fans were silent as the charismatic young woman onstage told them about her mother – how she had believed in her and worked four jobs, sacrificing everything for Selena's success. It was inspiring to hear Selena's story, to know that she had struggled.

"I live a very blessed life," Selena told her fans. "I have so much to be thankful for, and you are such a big part of inspiring me. You inspire me to be better. We should all inspire each other to be better."

The WE Day audience erupted into cheers. This was why they were here: these thousands of teens wanted to make the world a better place. WE Day was a global movement, all about taking action. It wasn't just grown-ups who could change the world! The kids in the audience had amazing ideas for making their communities, their cities, and even the world, better places. Seeing Selena onstage and hearing her powerful message had given them the strength to believe in themselves and what they could achieve.

Selena went on to explain about the pressure of fame: being told to look a certain way, behave a certain way... "I'm sure you can all relate. You all have pressure that you have to deal with every day."

Selena paused. Her expression was serious.

"Until recently, I had given in to that pressure. I lost sight of who I was. I tried to change who I am because I thought that others would accept me for it."

Now her voice cracked. Looking out at the sea of faces in front of her, Selena was on the verge of tears.

"And I realised that I don't know how to be anything but myself..."

Fans were hugging each other, crying, holding

the hands of the friends next to them. *Be yourself. Don't let anybody change you.* It was the message they wanted to hear. Their heroine was speaking to them like a friend, sharing her doubts and her anxieties.

"Please just be kind to each other," Selena continued. "Please stay true to yourself. Please just remain who you are and know that we have each other's backs. I've learned from my mistakes. I want you to know that I know what it's like. You are who you surround yourself with. I hope I can inspire you to trust yourself to love and to be loved."

"Let's change the game," Selena said. "This is such a beautiful thing that you're doing. Be proud of yourselves."